Cambridge Elements

Elements in Creativity and Imagination
edited by
Anna Abraham
University of Georgia, USA

PSYCHODRAMA

A Creative Method to Survive and Thrive

Hod Orkibi
University of Haifa

Shaftesbury Road, Cambridge CB2 8EA, United Kingdom

One Liberty Plaza, 20th Floor, New York, NY 10006, USA

477 Williamstown Road, Port Melbourne, VIC 3207, Australia

314–321, 3rd Floor, Plot 3, Splendor Forum, Jasola District Centre, New Delhi – 110025, India

103 Penang Road, #05-06/07, Visioncrest Commercial, Singapore 238467

Cambridge University Press is part of Cambridge University Press & Assessment, a department of the University of Cambridge.

We share the University's mission to contribute to society through the pursuit of education, learning and research at the highest international levels of excellence.

www.cambridge.org
Information on this title: www.cambridge.org/9781009571883

DOI: 10.1017/9781009378338

© Hod Orkibi 2025

This publication is in copyright. Subject to statutory exception and to the provisions of relevant collective licensing agreements, with the exception of the Creative Commons version the link for which is provided below, no reproduction of any part may take place without the written permission of Cambridge University Press & Assessment.

An online version of this work is published at doi.org/10.1017/9781009378338 under a Creative Commons Open Access license CC-BY-NC 4.0 which permits re-use, distribution and reproduction in any medium for non-commercial purposes providing appropriate credit to the original work is given and any changes made are indicated. To view a copy of this license visit https://creativecommons.org/licenses/by-nc/4.0

When citing this work, please include a reference to the DOI 10.1017/9781009378338

First published 2025

A catalogue record for this publication is available from the British Library

ISBN 978-1-009-57188-3 Hardback
ISBN 978-1-009-37830-7 Paperback
ISSN 2752-3950 (online)
ISSN 2752-3942 (print)

Cambridge University Press & Assessment has no responsibility for the persistence or accuracy of URLs for external or third-party internet websites referred to in this publication and does not guarantee that any content on such websites is, or will remain, accurate or appropriate.

For EU product safety concerns, contact us at Calle de José Abascal, 56, 1°, 28003 Madrid, Spain, or email eugpsr@cambridge.org

Psychodrama

A Creative Method to Survive and Thrive

Elements in Creativity and Imagination

DOI: 10.1017/9781009378338
First published online: July 2025

Hod Orkibi
University of Haifa
Author for correspondence: Hod Orkibi, horkibi@univ.haifa.ac.il

Abstract: This Element presents an integrated account of psychodrama theory, practice, and research. It begins by exploring psychodrama's psychosocial roots and emphasizes Jacob Levy Moreno's pioneering work. Core concepts such as spontaneity, creativity, adaptability, encounter, act-hunger, action insight, and act fulfillment are discussed in detail. This is followed by an overview of psychodrama practice, including session structure, core techniques, and a positive psychodrama intervention program. Five research designs for outcome studies are presented, along with key issues such as bias assessment, treatment fidelity, treatment differentiation, feasibility, and acceptability in psychodrama research. Change process research is reviewed in light of the latest evidence and methods, highlighting eleven therapeutic change factors in psychodrama and discussing concepts such as moderation, mediation, and mechanisms of change. The final section addresses future directions, including nonverbal synchrony and physiological and neurobiological pathways in psychodrama research. This title is also available as Open Access on Cambridge Core.

This Element also has a video abstract: www.cambridge.org/ECAI_Orkibi_abstract

Keywords: psychodrama, positive psychology, creativity, adaptability, spontaneity

© Hod Orkibi 2025

ISBNs: 9781009571883 (HB), 9781009378307 (PB), 9781009378338 (OC)
ISSNs: 2752-3950 (online), 2752-3942 (print)

Contents

1 Prelude   1

2 The Origins of Psychodrama   1

3 Core Concepts in Psychodrama   12

4 Psychodrama Practice: An Overview   19

5 Outcome Research: Does Psychodrama Work?   32

6 Change Process Research: How Does Psychodrama Work?   41

7 The Road Ahead   55

References   66

1 Prelude

*It Is Not the Strongest of the Species that Survives,
but the Most Adaptable to Change*

During my academic sabbatical year in February 2023, a psychodrama colleague posted this quote emphasizing the importance of adaptability for survival in changing environments. I later learned that many have misattributed this statement to Charles Darwin (1809–82), the British scientist who originated the theory of evolution by natural selection. In fact, the Darwin Correspondence Project, based at Cambridge University, classified this statement under "six things Darwin never said."[1] Nonetheless, I was captivated by this statement because it coincides with the thinking of Jacob Levy Moreno (1889–1974), the creator of psychodrama, as manifested in his magnum opus *Who Shall Survive?* (Moreno, 1934, p. 898). Moreno's central argument is that those who survive are flexible, spontaneous, and creative within "a well-integrated society" that has strong and positive social bonds (p. 366). In a later essay, Moreno specified that "people must be creative in order to survive" because "the more creative the personality, the more problems it can solve, and that the more creative it is, the better it can structure and predict the future . . ." (Moreno, 1964, pp. 158–159). The purpose of psychodrama is to unlock people's spontaneity and creativity, helping them navigate life with greater adaptability. This aligns with the principles of positive psychology and resonates with the World Health Organization's definition of health as "a state of complete physical, mental and social well-being and not merely the absence of disease or infirmity" (World Health Organization, 1948). Complete health, therefore, involves not only surviving but also thriving.

2 The Origins of Psychodrama

Before delving into the origins of psychodrama, some context and definitions are needed. Psychodrama can be regarded as one of the creative arts therapies (CATs), an umbrella term covering health professions that use the creative and expressive processes of art engagement and its outcomes in psychodrama, drama therapy,[2] art therapy, dance movement therapy, music therapy, and poetry/bibliotherapy. Creative arts therapists undergo extensive education

---

[1] www.darwinproject.ac.uk/people/about-darwin/six-things-darwin-never-said#quote1.
[2] Drama therapy is a CATs discipline that uses theater processes and techniques within a therapeutic relationship. In drama therapy, the story and characters are mostly imaginary, symbolic, and fantasy-based, whereas in psychodrama, they are mostly reality-based. Drama therapy may culminate in a performance, whereas psychodrama is process-oriented and does not involve performance. Drama therapy encompasses different methods developed by several founders in the US and the UK, whereas psychodrama has one cohesive method developed by J. L. Moreno and Zerka T. Moreno.

and clinical training to prepare them to apply arts-based methods and creative processes to optimize health and well-being within a formal therapeutic relationship. They work with individuals of all ages, couples, families, and groups across various mental health, medical, rehabilitation, educational, and community settings (de Witte et al., 2021).

Psychodrama is an experiential therapy originated by J. L. Moreno in the early 1920s and developed by his third wife, Zerka Toema Moreno (1917–2016), a Dutch-born American psychotherapist. Psychodramatists employ guided role-play and specific techniques to address personal and interpersonal issues, facilitate insight, change, and integration on the cognitive, emotional, behavioral, and social levels (Orkibi & Feniger-Schaal, 2019; Orkibi et al., 2023). Psychodrama offers protagonists a "failsafe" space where their feelings, thoughts, and behaviors can be explored in action rather than words alone, and insights can be gained into past issues, present challenges, and future possibilities (Orkibi, 2019). The following sections provide a brief overview of the origins of psychodrama, from developmental psychology, through shamanism and Moreno's early theatrical work, to psychodrama as a recognized mental health profession.

2.1 Developmental and Psychosocial Roots

Drama can be traced back to pretend play in childhood. *Pretend play*[3] is a term used in the literature to describe an imaginative play where children engage in make-believe roles and scenarios, often attributing meanings to objects beyond their literal or immediate context (Pellegrini et al., 2007). Children exhibit this natural and universal behavior, but its quantity and quality differ significantly across cultures (Taylor, 2013, p. 224). It can take several forms including solitary play (involving objects and imaginary others), play with an adult, and play with peers (Frahsek et al., 2010; Russ, 2014). Developmentally, pretend play typically begins with object substitution—where one object is mentally or physically used to represent another—around twelve to eighteen months of age. It peaks between the ages of three and five with the use of pretend identities and scenarios, and generally declines by around eleven years (Lillard, 2017).

2.1.1 Moreno's Theory of Child Development

In Moreno's *spontaneity theory of child development*, pregnancy is viewed as a warm-up for both mother and fetus that culminates in the cathartic moment of birth, which he described as "a primary and creative process. It is positive before

---

[3] Also termed "sociodramatic play."

it is negative, it is healthy before it is pathological, it is a victory before it is a trauma" (Moreno, 1978, p. 42). Birth, therefore, is not a traumatic event but rather a victorious culmination of nine months of preparation. At birth, the newborn undergoes a profound transition from the confines of the womb to boundless openness, from darkness to a vibrant, illuminated world, from complete dependence on the mother's nourishment to some level of self-initiated feeding. This abrupt shift requires rapid adaptation as the infant navigates new sights, sounds, and movements. Thus, for Moreno, the instant of birth represents the peak of readiness for the spontaneous act of entering a new environment that demands swift adaptation.

Unlike other vertebrates, human newborns are not self-sufficient. Human infants enter a complex and hazardous world before they are fully prepared, with an underdeveloped body and brain requiring extensive nurturing to survive. Moreno argued that the newborn goes through "changes from a situation which provides him [sic] with a safe equilibrium to a world which is to be conquered if he is to survive in it ..." (Moreno & Moreno, 1944, p. 92). Nevertheless, in contrast to other theories of his time (e.g., Freud), Moreno argued that his theory conceptualizes the infant's growth in *positive* terms of progression and achievements rather than in negative terms of retardation and regression (Moreno & Moreno, 1944, p. 109). He emphasized the crucial role of spontaneity (the "S factor") in enabling the infant to navigate experiences and situations for the first time, by likening the infant to an impromptu actor who explores uncharted scenarios (Moreno & Moreno, 1944).

The theory consists of three phases (Moreno, 2006).[4] The *first phase*, the "matrix of all-identity," is an egocentric state where infants perceive themselves as inseparable from the universe (similar to the Freudian concept of age-appropriate primary narcissism), with no differentiation between people, animals, and objects or between the representation of objects (reflected images) and their actual nature. In this phase, all impulses are directed inward toward the infant, and most of the time, infants alternate between short periods of wakefulness and sleep. Thus, their experiences are predominantly physiological in nature, that is, not driven by conscious motives. Infants' complete absorption in their current activity is the main reason for the underdevelopment of the past and future time dimensions and the centrality of the present moment, the here-and-now.

In the *second phase* of "differentiated all-identities," infants start to differentiate between people, animals, and objects but are still unaware that they do not

---

[4] In the first paper on the spontaneity theory of child development, J. L. Moreno and his wife at the time, Florence B. Moreno (1944), described five phases, which were later revised to three phases by his third wife Zerka T. Moreno (2006).

control them, and there is still no differentiation between fantasy and reality. Infants notice their mother (or primary caretaker) but do not yet understand that they are separate entities and still experience her as a dual entity in which they and their mother are one in a symbiotic relationship. The first and the second phases unfold in what Moreno calls the "first universe" of the infant.

In the *third phase*, which takes place in the "second universe," typically around the age of three, young children become increasingly capable of forming mental representations of objects, experiences, and concepts, leading to the development of a distinction between fantasy and reality (Moreno & Moreno, 1944). This developmental shift is linked to cognitive maturation, which involves improved memory, language skills, and an emerging theory of mind that enables children to attribute mental states to themselves and others. As these abilities grow, so does the capacity to distinguish between imagination and reality, though some blurring may persist in early childhood, particularly during play and storytelling (Harris, 2000). According to Moreno and Moreno (1944), this phase constitutes a profound existential shock as children begin to grasp the boundaries between their imagined world and actual reality. This realization can be unsettling since it challenges their previously fluid perception of reality and imagination. Zerka T. Moreno (2006) later argued that "the organism of the child is driven by a hunger for action . . . he [*sic*] hungers to know what is going on about him, who and what is out there. He also wants to define his own position in space and to be affirmed as an entity" (p. 55). Note that Moreno's theory of child development does not specify months or years for each phase and is more of a conceptual framework associated with psychodrama practice, as discussed in Section 4.3.

2.1.2 Moreno's Role Theory

Moreno's developmental theory is closely tied to his role theory. Like a spontaneous actor, the infant takes on a new role where each step into the world generates novel experiences (Moreno & Moreno, 1944, p. 109). Broadly speaking, the three core premises of the theory are that (a) roles precede the self, with one's sense of self emerging from and being structured by the dynamic interaction of the roles one plays in life; (b) the tangible/visible aspects of the self are the roles in which one operates in a specific situation; and (c) every individual has a range of roles, where having a broader role repertoire enables the individual to act flexibly and adequately, in the right way at the right time, with greater adaptability and thus better mental health (Moreno, 1962).

The first developmental phase is dominated by *psychosomatic roles*, physiological roles related to the infant's primary biological needs for survival (e.g., breathing, sleeping, nursing, urinating, defecating, crying, crawling, etc.). Two other types of roles develop after the distinction between fantasy (psychodrama) and reality (society) is consolidated. *Psychodramatic roles* are psychological roles that develop in relation to inner mental and emotional experiences, including roles rooted in memories and in anticipation of the future, hopes, and fears. These roles associate psychological, imaginative, and dramatic contexts with experiences that expand beyond the constraints of ordinary physical reality. *Social roles* are those developed in relation to a function in real life. Examples of social roles include parent, child, sibling, teacher, friend, student, therapist, researcher, and so on. However, it is important to note that every role is a blend of personal and collective elements, such that a role consists of two components: its collective aspects shared with others and its individual differentiating characteristics (Moreno & Moreno, 1944). Moreno (1962) proposed that a unified self evolves from a dynamic self-creative process in which the body, psyche, and society are integrated. In short, "role is a fusion of private and collective elements. It is a unit of 'conserved' behavior (one form of cultural conserve)" (Hare & Hare, 1996, p. 37). In essence, "Moreno's *role theory* bridges the individual and the community, psychology and sociology, as it examines intrapersonal (intrapsychic) phenomena as well as interpersonal (interpsychic) interactions" (Lelkes, 2021, p. 147).

A person interacts with a given role in four distinct ways, each reflecting progressively higher levels of spontaneity, freedom of personal choice, and variation in how the role is expressed. *Role-taking* is the act of observing and emulating a model's actions, behaviors, or processes. Modeling is one of the deepest forms of learning. It focuses on reproducing the outwardly visible aspects of behavior without necessarily understanding its motivation, purpose, or consequences. Role-taking is the conscious or unconscious taking on of a fully established conserved role with no degrees of freedom or individual variation. By contrast, *role-playing* is the act of engaging in what was learned in role-taking, but this time involves inserting oneself into the new role one is playing and experimenting with, and making adaptations to the role, with limited degrees of freedom. Moreno reasoned that role-taking and role-playing go hand in hand in a primary learning and conditioning process that cannot be separated. In *role-creating*, elements of the first two stages are maintained while creating a new role that corresponds to one's talents, needs, and desires, with a high degree of freedom (Moreno & Moreno, 1944). *Role-training* involves using role-play to practice or rehearse a specific role to perform adequately in future situations (Blatner, 2000a; Moreno, 1994, p. 63) – for example, being more assertive or compassionate.

Blatner (1991) suggested that Moreno's idea of using the role concept to represent a problem or behavior is more understandable, practical, less pathologizing, and less stigmatizing than labeling individuals as having psychiatric disorders. In other words, the conceptualization of problems as roles acknowledges that none of these roles defines the person exclusively. It allows protagonists to differentiate themselves from their problems (i.e., maladaptive roles), step back, and reflect on their actions while adopting what Blatner (2006) termed the *meta-role*, which serves as the coordinator of all the other roles in one's repertoire. The meta-role, therefore, is the inner playwright/director, the "choosing self" role that can re-author or re-direct a situation to reevaluate, redefine, and modify the different roles people play in life (Blatner, 2000a). Thus, the concept of the meta-role facilitates self-awareness, a sense of self-control, and adaptation (Azoulay & Orkibi, 2015).

According to Clayton (1994), recognizing one's role repertoire allows for the freedom to consciously choose roles that align with one's current emotions and values, thereby fostering greater authenticity (Lelkes, 2021, p. 148). Mapping a person's *role system* can promote optimal role balance, support the resolution of internal conflicts, and expand the repertoire of adaptive responses to various life situations. Lelkes (2021), a student of Clayton, defined six types of roles. *Adequate roles* are well-balanced and appropriately enacted to meet situational needs, which contribute positively to overall functioning and well-being. *Underdeveloped roles* are present but not fully formed or utilized, leading to limited effectiveness or unrealized potential. *Excessive roles* dominate a person's behavior to an extreme degree, overshadowing other essential roles and causing imbalance. *Absent roles* are completely missing from a person's behavior or personality, often leading to a lack of certain skills or perspectives. *Saboteur roles* actively undermine a person's efforts and well-being, often resulting in self-destructive or harmful behaviors. In short, this analytic approach is designed to help individuals recognize, refine, and expand their role repertoire, ultimately promoting adaptation and a greater capacity for thriving. For psychodramatic applications, see Lelkes (2021).

2.1.3 Related Perspectives on Child Development

Several prominent scholars have contributed to a better understanding of the psycho-developmental origins of children's play. *Lev Vygotsky* (1896–1934), a Russian psychologist, claimed that play, especially with others, takes place within the child's *zone of proximal development* situated between children's actual developmental level (what the child can do independently) and their potential developmental level (what the child can do with guidance or assistance from a more skillful person). Within this play zone, children engage in activities beyond their current developmental abilities with the help of peers, siblings, caregivers, teachers, and so on. This plays a crucial role in developing language, communication, socio-emotional skills, and the acquisition of cultural knowledge such as norms and values (Vygotsky, 1966). Another prominent play scholar was the Dutch historian and cultural theorist *Johan Huizinga* (1872–1945), who argued that play is not merely a voluntary, frivolous and joyful activity but rather an essential element in laying the foundation for the development of human culture and civilization (Huizinga, 1944). He suggested that play occurs within a realm that is separate from everyday reality. It is distinguished by its volitional "disinterested" nature, in that play is pursued for its intrinsic value rather than for any utilitarian or physical reward. Unlike animal play, human play is distinguished by the capacity for symbolism, a trait pervasive across creative domains (e.g., theater), which thus nurtures and stimulates creative imagination. *Jean Piaget* (1896–1980), a Swiss psychologist, posited that play is essential to children's cognitive development because children actively construct knowledge about themselves and the world through play experiences. Through various stages of development, children engage in different types of play, such as sensorimotor play, pretend play, and games with rules that contribute to problem-solving skills and abstract thinking (Piaget, 1962). Finally, the British pediatrician and psychoanalyst *Donald Winnicott* (1896–1971) considered that play is a creative and spontaneous activity that takes place in what he called a *potential space* – an intermediate psychological zone between the inner world (fantasy) and the external reality where children can process and communicate their inner emotions, thoughts, and fantasies freely in a nonthreatening and symbolic way (Winnicott, 1980). Winnicott argued that playful activities, when facilitated by caregivers who provide a supportive and safe "holding environment," help children make sense of their experiences, develop a sense of agency, and foster problem-solving and the exploration of new ideas.

2.1.4 Social Perspectives

Social psychologists primarily view roles as related to social interactions (Callero, 1994; Mead, 1967; Sarbin & Allen, 1968). In the dramaturgical approach to social psychology, "drama is used as a way of understanding the nature of the self. People are termed as actors in everyday life and the way people relate to each other is described dramaturgically; that is, in dramatic terms" (Jones, 2007, p. 41). Goffman (1973) used the performance metaphor to account for interpersonal interactions in his seminal book *The Presentation of Self in Everyday Life*. As natural performers, people employ dramaturgical techniques and strategies for impression management in the presence of others. The performer's task is to overcome performance disruption (by the self or others), maintain expressive control, and present convincing character coherence. Thus, one must possess dramaturgical loyalty, discipline, and circumspection to produce a successful self-presentation. As Goffman (1973, p. 72) argued, almost anyone can act in "some sense of realness . . . . because ordinary social intercourse is itself put together as a [theatrical] scene is put together. Scripts, even in the hands of unpracticed players, can come to life because life itself is a dramatically enacted thing." The performative nature of people's existence is also intensified by the contemporary domination of reality TV and the pervasive use of photos and videos for self-presentation in social media and the online world (see Schechner & Brady, 2013).

Thus, as an art form, drama may appear highly user-friendly because it is intuited in the performative "practice" of everyday life, where people play various roles and interpersonal interactions are inherently dramatic and performative. Life as self-presentation hence seems to provide for intuitive, tacit, personal knowledge of role-playing or acting (Orkibi, 2018). Drama therapist Robert Landy (1982) proposed that "the expressive art of spontaneous drama is for all, as we are all performers in everyday life" (p. 96). Landy further suggested that "all human beings have the inherent dramatic need to perform and to be applauded for their performance . . . . [because] we all want to be stars; we all want recognition" (p. 96). In short, dramaturgical perspectives coincide with the line from Shakespeare's *As You Like It* (Act II, Scene VII): "All the world's a stage, and all the men and women merely players."

2.2 Anthropological Perspectives: Shamanism

Shamanism is a spiritual and religious practice that has existed in diverse cultures worldwide for thousands of years (Eliade, 1972). The specific practices and beliefs associated with shamanism vary widely from culture to culture. Shamans commonly serve as healers in their communities through the enactment of performative rituals and ceremonies, which have long been considered the forerunners of theater and performance (Kirby, 1974). This view aligns, to some extent, with the School of Cambridge approach, which posits that ancient rituals were the origin of Greek tragedy and comedy (Rozik, 2002).

Within a broader context, some scholars have identified shamanic elements in the CATs (McNiff, 1979; Moreno, 1988; Schmais, 1988). More specifically, shamanism has been seen as a precursor of drama therapy, since both shamans and drama therapists facilitate entry into an imaginal world for healing and transformation, and both employ dramatic/theatrical elements in ritual and symbolic actions to achieve this purpose (Glaser, 2004; Pendzik, 1988). Both shamanism and drama therapy establish distinct temporal and spatial boundaries, separate from ordinary reality (Casson, 2016; Jennings, 1995). In addition, both practices place significant emphasis on inducing profound emotional experiences: shamanic rituals evoke states of ecstasy or trances, whereas psychodrama and drama therapy may involve catharsis (Moreno, 1940). Crucially, however, although shamanism and drama-based therapies share elements of ritual, imagination, and healing, they have different cultural contexts and historical backgrounds. Unlike shamans, psychodramatists and drama therapists rely on conventional mental health evidence and do not attribute mental illness to supernatural beliefs, nor do they enter into a trance themselves or propel their clients into one (Snow, 2009). Whereas shamanism is a spiritual and healing practice rooted in various indigenous cultures worldwide, psychodrama and drama therapy are modern therapeutic methods with growing empirical evidence supporting their benefits for health and well-being (Feniger-Schaal & Orkibi, 2020; Orkibi & Feniger-Schaal, 2019; Orkibi et al., 2023).

2.3 Early Portrayals of Therapeutic Drama

Early portrayals of therapeutic drama can be found in plays from the Jacobean era (1603–25), where drama elements were used to treat the characters' mental health conditions. In *Hamlet* and *King Lear*, Shakespeare alluded to the therapeutic potential of drama. In contrast, in his last play, *The Two Noble Kinsmen* (1613–14), he clearly portrayed a doctor who uses drama to treat a woman with psychotic delusions (Casson, 2006). Several other playwrights from the Jacobean era also wrote about the healing effects of drama (Casson, 2007a, 2007b), thus suggesting that "plays demonstrated that theater could be therapy three hundred years before the emergence of dramatherapy and psychodrama" (Casson, 2007a, p. 9).

During the eighteenth century, Philippe Pinel (1745–1826), the founder of enlightened psychiatry in France, and Johann Christian Reil (1759–1813), a prominent German physician who coined the term 'psychiatry,' introduced theater as a method of treatment of mental illness (Casson, 1997). In his *Rhapsodies on the Application of Psychic Cure Method of Mental Disorders*, Reil (1803) argued that "therapeutic theater could aid individual cases in a variety of diseases ... [and] may help the patient to eliminate his [*sic*] fixed ideas or his misdirected emotions" (as cited in Harms, 1957, p. 807). Another prominent figure of this time was J. W. von Goethe (1749–1832), a German poet, novelist, statesman, and scientist whose idea of treating mental illness can be inferred from his Singspiel *Lila*, a musical drama where a woman of this name is cured of her delusions by family members and friends who participate in a therapeutic enactment prescribed by her doctor (Goethe, 1788/1973). As Moreno stated, "No other playwright has constructed an entire play, that is, every scene, every word, the entire structure of the play, to demonstrate drama itself as cure" (Moreno, 2010, p. 123). In a previous work, I identified psychodramatic elements and techniques in Goethe's *Lila* (Orkibi, 2009).

2.4 Moreno's Early Experiments

Prior to and during the time he was a medical student at the University of Vienna (1911–17), J. L. Moreno experimented with storytelling and role-playing in the parks of Vienna, where he was fascinated by children's inherent spontaneity and creativity (Moreno, 1964). This was also when Moreno's work with groups of female sex workers (1913–14) from Vienna's "red light district" gave rise to the idea of group therapy.[5] As part of a project to curb the spread of venereal disease and organize sex workers into a labor union, he held meetings with groups of eight to ten sex workers several times a week, accompanied by a physician specializing in venereal disease and the publisher of a Viennese newspaper (Moreno, 1953). The focus gradually switched from discussions on various health issues to therapeutic interactions to address their personal suffering, as "gradually they recognized the deeper value of the meetings, that they could help each other" (Moreno, 2019, p. 36). In retrospect, Moreno considered that these activities with children and sex workers were the forerunners of psychodrama: "Psychodrama was done in life, on the streets, in the parks, and in the homes. We had no psychodrama stage then. The theatrical element was implicit rather than explicit. The participants were real people and the problems were real ..." (Moreno & Moreno, 2012, p. 30).

2.5 From Improvisational to Therapeutic Theater

Contrary to popular belief, conventional theater did not give rise to psychodrama. In fact, Moreno criticized the conventional theater of his time, calling it "a rigid drama conserve" – in other words, the culmination of a finished creative process (Moreno, 1994, p. 39). He claimed that by adopting a fictional character's identity, conventional theater actors dehumanized and diminished their own selves. Instead of being preoccupied with mimesis and scripted situations, Moreno was interested in life itself. He viewed drama as an extension of life, not an imitation (Moreno, 1994), and was therefore interested in facilitating a real-life spontaneous existential *encounter* in the here-and-now (J. L. Moreno,

---

[5] J. L. Moreno is credited with coining the term "group therapy" at the 1931 conference of the American Psychiatric Association in New York City.

1969a) – that is, a deep and direct interpersonal communication that involves reversing roles with others, with all their strengths and weaknesses (Moreno, 1960, 1964). He used the Latin terms *locus nascendi*, *status nascendi*, and *matrix to* emphasize the importance of understanding the interconnectedness of origin, process, and environment in fostering growth and transformation (Moreno, 1994). *Locus nascendi* refers to the specific starting point or origin ("birthplace") of a new idea, action, insight, or psychological wound. *Status nascendi*, by contrast, describes the dynamic and evolving process of creation as it unfolds at a particular time. Both are supported by the *matrix*, which provides the relational and contextual foundation that nurtures and shapes the experience, and serves as the 'social womb' from which it emerges (Moreno, 1994).

In 1922, Moreno founded the Viennese Theater of Spontaneity (Das Stegreiftheater) to fulfill his vision of facilitating an existential encounter (J. L. Moreno, 1969b) and to liberate the conventional theater of his time from predetermined content and form. This theater abandoned written scripts and the stage to transform the actors and the audience into improvising co-creators (Moreno, 2010, p. 12). Role-playing was frequently cathartic and healing for the players as they experimented with different forms of improvised theater. One momentous event is the story of Barbara, a young actress in Moreno's theater who played angelic, sweet, and romantic roles but was, according to her husband, verbally and physically abusive toward him at home (Moreno, 1994). Barbara's abusive behavior became shorter and less frequent after several sessions where Moreno cast her into new roles in which she had the opportunity to express and discharge her aggression in the as-if reality on stage. Moreno pointed to this event as one of the roots of psychodrama.

The public and the press were generally opposed to the Theater of Spontaneity because they had little appreciation for impromptu performances despite occasional positive reviews and brief moments of success. Moreno realized that "a hundred percent spontaneity in a therapeutic theater was easier to advocate; the aesthetic imperfections of an actor could not be forgiven, but the imperfections and incongruities a mental patient might show on the stage were not only more easily tolerated but expected and often warmly welcomed" (Moreno, 2010, p. 22). Consequently, the Theater of Spontaneity became the Therapeutic Theater, also called the Theater of Catharsis.

2.6 Psychodrama as a Profession

Although Moreno first used the term "psychodrama" in 1919 (J. L. Moreno, 1969b, p. 15), it was only after his immigration to the United States in 1925 that his experiments with audience participation evolved into a structured therapeutic method (Blatner, 2000a). Most techniques used in classical psychodrama gradually developed from 1936 into the early 1940s (Blatner, 2000a). In 1942, Moreno founded the American Society of Group Psychotherapy and Psychodrama (https://asgpp.org). It has been argued that given Moreno's background in psychiatry, psychodrama "began to stray from the aesthetics of its theatrical roots" (Emunah & Johnson, 2009, p. 5). This difference between psychodrama's theatrical roots and its actual practice may have contributed to the emergence of drama therapy in the United States (Emunah & Johnson, 2009). In some countries, psychodrama is regarded as one of the CATs (e.g., in Israel, and to some extent in the United States), while in others, it is considered a form of humanistic and/or group psychotherapy (e.g., in the UK and Austria).[6] Today, psychodrama is also used in nontherapeutic fields such as in organizations (Orkibi, 2023b), education (Marra et al., 2022), and with trial lawyers (Leach, 2003).

3 Core Concepts in Psychodrama

This section provides an overview of core concepts in the theoretical framework of psychodrama as put forth by J. L. Moreno, who developed his theory unsystematically and inconsistently. Boria (1989) claimed that the theoretical framework of psychodrama is more of a foundation awaiting further development. Hence, psychodrama theory consists of a combination of rich, complex, and interrelated theoretical concepts rather than a coherent doctrine (Bustos, 1994). As a result, some psychodrama practitioners align their practice with Moreno's theory, whereas others opt for a theory-free approach that views psychodrama as a collection of techniques applicable to various psychotherapeutic or theoretical perspectives (Wilkins, 1999). Similarly, Kellermann (1987a) contended that psychodrama should be defined in a manner that does not presuppose a specific theoretical orientation. Blatner (1996) also argued that psychodrama is better characterized as a praxis rather than a distinct school of thought, "a complex of both technique and the principles which underlie their application" (p. 157). However, Moreno argued against separating his method from its underlying philosophy, as is evident from his statement: "Take my ideas, my concepts, but do not separate them from their parent, the philosophy; do not split my children in half, like a Solomonic judgement. Love them in toto, support and respect the entire structure upon which they rest . . ." (cited in Z. T. Moreno, 1969a, p. 5).

---

[6] See the Federation of European Psychodrama Training Organizations (FEPTO), which assembles organizations from European and Mediterranean countries to advance psychodrama training. www.fepto.com/.

3.1 Surplus Reality

Psychodramatic processes and techniques manifest what Moreno called *surplus reality*, a subjective reality that goes beyond ordinary reality, where protagonists can actively explore personal and interpersonal concerns and their innermost feared and hoped-for past, present, and future scenarios (J. L. Moreno, 1965). Moreno believed that "he could not truly meet the psyche of the protagonist unless he [*sic*] lived in the surplus reality together with the protagonist" and that "it is not until you have been interviewed and warmed-up into action that you go into surplus reality" (Moreno et al., 2000, pp. 18–20). Surplus reality transcends the boundaries of ordinary reality (including sex, age, death, time, and place), thus enabling the protagonists to engage with re-presented, imagined, or symbolic enactments that extend beyond their actual lived experiences. Moreno drew inspiration from Karl Marx's concept of surplus value;[7] however, rather than emphasizing economic loss, surplus reality facilitates therapeutic gains. Note that the concept of surplus reality corresponds to similar ideas, such as fantastic reality (Rubinstein & Lahad, 2023), dramatic reality (Pendzik, 2006), and potential space (Winnicott, 1980), all of which address the interplay between one's imagination and lived experience in facilitating psychological growth.

3.2 Spontaneity, Creativity, and Adaptability

The two inseparable core concepts in psychodrama are spontaneity and creativity, which Moreno viewed as "*primary* and *positive* phenomena" in contrast to the Freudian view of his time that humans are inherently savage animals, prone to swift and violent behavior unless controlled by civilization, physical, and legal coercion (Moreno, 1994, p. 49). For Moreno, *spontaneity* is a pre-creative catalyzing *state of readiness* through which creativity emerges (Moreno, 1955b, p. 365), such that spontaneity is actualized through creative acts (Kipper, 1986, p. 13). Formally, Moreno defined spontaneity as a state of readiness that propels "the individual towards an *adequate* response to a new situation or a *new* response to an old situation" (Moreno, 1953, p. 42, emphases added). The adequacy of a response is a function of its suitability to the requirements of a given situation (Moreno, 1994, p. 93). An adequate response is made "with competency and skill" (Hare & Hare, 1996, p. 36) and is "*well-timed,* and

---

[7] *Surplus value* is a core concept in Marx's critique of capitalism. He argued that it is the source of profit in capitalist systems that is generated through the exploitation of labor. Workers not only receive less compensation than the value they produce but effectively lose money, since the unpaid surplus value of their labor is appropriated by capitalists and becomes the foundation for the accumulation of capital.

neither too much nor too little in *intensity*" (Kipper, 1986, p. 12). The newness of response refers to being "fresh, novel, creative, in the here and now, not foreordained or predetermined, but arising out of the immediate situation ..." (Z. T. Moreno, 1969b, p. 213). Thus, spontaneity is not conservable, cannot be accumulated or stored, and is spent as it emerges and operates solely in the immediate moment (Moreno, 1955b). Unlike its everyday meaning, and supported by empirical findings (Kipper et al., 2010), spontaneity in psychodrama is different from mindless instinctive or uninhibited impulsivity since it moves in a prescribed direction and therefore contains an element of self-control (Kipper, 1986, p. 11), autonomy, and freedom from uncontrollable external or internal influences (Moreno, 1941, pp. 213–214). Taken together, Moreno believed that because spontaneity typically decreases with age (Moreno, 1994, p. 80) and is often discouraged, restrained, or feared (Moreno, 1974, p. 80), the purpose of psychodrama is to restore and release it. Although every individual has an innate capacity for spontaneity and its resulting creativity, this capacity needs to be warmed up in psychodrama through four preconditions: a sense of trust and safety; openness to intuition, images, feelings, and nonrational processes; playfulness; and a movement toward risk-taking and exploration (Blatner, 1996, p. 43). Moreno (1978) described the warming-up process as "the operational expression of spontaneity" (p. 42), which fosters creativity, facilitates change, and enables new ways of responding to and engaging with the world. Thus, establishing a safe environment for warm-up is an essential precondition for spontaneity, which, in turn, fuels creativity. Several studies have reported positive associations between spontaneity and well-being, extraversion, self-actualization, creative capacity, and playfulness, and negative associations with stress, anxiety, depression, neuroticism, and symptoms of obsessive-compulsive disorder (Biancalani & Orkibi, 2025; Christoforou & Kipper, 2006; Kellar et al., 2002; Kipper & Hundal, 2005; Kipper & Shemer, 2006; Tarashoeva et al., 2017).

By contrast, creativity can only emerge if it is catalyzed by a state of spontaneity. This means that creativity is the creative outcome, whether in the form of a creative product (e.g., a poem or a smartphone) or as a psychological response. In this context, Moreno used the concept of the *Godhead* as a theological metaphor for an infinite wellspring of creation from which all existence emerges in the cosmos[8] (Moreno, 1955a, 1972). Inspired by the Jewish mystical tradition of Kabbalah, Moreno viewed people as cosmo-dynamic

---

[8] The term "cosmos" has metaphorical and philosophical connotations that emphasize an ordered and harmonious universe. It underscores the interconnectedness of all things and conveys a holistic, integrated perspective. In contrast, the term "universe" refers more broadly to the entirety of space, time, and matter without necessarily implying order or harmony.

beings, sharing a *co-creative* power with the supreme creator and actively participating in the creative dynamics of the cosmos (Moreno & Moreno, 2012, p. 23). Therefore, Moreno's "I-God" concept stands for "I-Creator" and must not be confused with superiority or egotism and should not be related to any religious context (Moreno, 1955a, p. 391). This third model of the human-God relationship contrasts with the first "He-God" model in the Old Testament, where God is invisible, and the second "Thou-God" model of the New Testament, where God is a loving human being (Marineau, 1989). Instead, Moreno's "I-God" concept reflects a belief in the godlikeness of each individual (Moreno, 2010, p. 26) to the extent that "each person is both the one who creates and the one who is created and is therefore responsible for the world which they have created and everyone and everything in it" (Tauvon, 1998, p. 31). In other words, people are co-responsible with each other for themselves and the entire world. As mentioned in the Prelude, Moreno (1964) argued that "people must be creative in order to survive" because "the more creative the personality, the more problems it can solve, and that the more creative it is, the better it can structure and predict the future . . ." (pp. 158–159). Thus, creativity is essential for adapting to life changes and unexpected challenges.

Inspired by this stance, I developed the concept of *creative adaptability*, which refers to one's ability to respond creatively and adaptively to stressful and/or changed/new situations (Orkibi, 2021, 2023a). Creative adaptability is thus a personal resource that involves the ability to generate personally new and potentially effective cognitive, behavioral, and emotional responses that may lead to positive outcomes. Cognitive creative adaptability refers to generating personally new and potentially effective ideas, perspectives, and thoughts. Behavioral creative adaptability refers to executing personally new and potentially effective behaviors and actions. Emotional creative adaptability refers to generating personally new and potentially effective emotional reactions.

Although the traditional bipartite definition of creativity affirms that creativity entails generating outcomes that are both *novel* (new, original, unique) and *effective* (adaptive, appropriate, useful) (Runco & Jaeger, 2012), the concepts of novelty and effectiveness are not absolute. Judgments of whether creative ideas, solutions, or products are new and effective are often made by experts in a specific domain (Kaufman & Baer, 2012). However, within the context of creative adaptability, determining whether a response is new, as opposed to routine or habitual, depends on the individual's viewpoint. Similar to Runco's theory of personal creativity (Runco, 1996, 2011), the creativity in creative adaptability does not necessarily demand an external reference. Instead, it is considered new based on an internal frame of reference that takes the individual's past experiences in a particular context into account. The effectiveness of a response is assessed by its ability to optimize positive outcomes and minimize negative ones. Nonetheless, the actual effectiveness of a response can sometimes be reevaluated in hindsight, as it depends not only on foresight but also on retrospective insight (Averill, 2005; Averill et al., 2001). This perspective aligns with the "1.5" criterion model of creativity, where novelty represents the "1" criterion, while the "0.5" indicates that an idea need only possess the potential for usefulness or effectiveness to be considered creative; hence 0.5 instead of 1 (Smith & Smith, 2017). In the context of creative adaptability, the 0.5 criterion implies that a response should, at minimum, be potentially effective by explicitly providing benefits to individuals experiencing stress in a given context. Accumulating evidence suggests that creative adaptability (as measured by the creative adaptability scale) predicts and is associated with a range of well-being indices (Orkibi, 2021, 2023a; Orkibi et al., 2024). A study designed to develop and provide an initial validation of a new *State Spontaneity Scale* found that creative adaptability was moderately related to state spontaneity (Biancalani & Orkibi, 2025), which is consistent with Moreno's conceptualization that the two constructs are related but distinct. In addition, as theorized, both constructs were negatively correlated with state anxiety.

3.3 Interpersonal Encounters and the Flourishing of Humanity

Moreno's concept of the "social and organic unity of mankind" suggests that human society functions as an interconnected system (Moreno, 1953, p. 3). He proposed that individuals in society are not isolated entities but rather integral parts of a larger social organism. This perspective emphasizes that individuals' actions, behaviors, and relationships contribute to the functioning and well-being of society as a whole. It also highlights the importance of understanding and addressing social dynamics, relationships, and structures in promoting individual and collective well-being.

Moreno had "faith in our fellowmen's [sic] intentions . . . . [and viewed] love and mutual sharing as a powerful, indispensable working principle in group life" (Moreno, 1953, p. xv). He believed that humans are inherently social beings who are born with a natural inclination toward altruism and concern for the well-being of others as well as their own in what he considered a relational world. Therefore, expressing spontaneity and creativity within authentic interpersonal relationships is crucial for the flourishing of humanity (Blatner & Cukier, 2007, p. 294). Moreno thus believed that people should be treated in groups rather than alone in isolation, and put forward the concept of *sociatry* to convey his interest in the well-being not only of individuals (i.e., psychiatry) but of groups, communities, and society as a whole (Moreno, 1978,

p. 119). Moreno aimed for a "society in which our deepest selves are realized" (Moreno, 1949, p. 236) and believed that "a truly therapeutic procedure cannot have less an objective than the whole of mankind" (Moreno, 1978, p. 3).

Moreno believed that human potential is fully actualized through relationships with others, not in isolation, by genuinely considering the 'You' alongside the 'I' in interpersonal existential encounters in the here-and-now (Moreno, 1949, p. 238). An *encounter* (in German: Begegnung) is a profound interpersonal meeting and form of communication that involves role reversal and creates a direct and authentic connection between the self and others with both strengths and weaknesses (Moreno, 1960, 1964). Moreno went so far as to state that his entire triadic system – sociometry, psychodrama, and group psychotherapy – serves as an instrument to facilitate interpersonal encounters (J. L. Moreno, 1969b).

At this point, it is worth briefly mentioning two other methods developed by Moreno. The first is *sociometry*, defined as the systematic, action-based study and measurement of covert and overt patterns of social relationships, choices, and dynamics within a group or a community (Moreno, 1942). Sociometry highlights these patterns and provides insights into their influence on individuals, cohesion, and overall productivity (Moreno, 1953) while emphasizing the interconnectedness of individuals and reflecting Moreno's broader interest in the interconnectedness of society. *Sociodrama*,[9] on the other hand, utilizes improvisational role-playing techniques to explore socio-political and intercultural issues, as well as societal power dynamics and processes (Moreno, 1943). Thus, whereas psychodrama focuses on the individual and sociometry focuses on relationships between individuals, sociodrama focuses on the group as a whole, by exploring sociodramatic roles that embody collective ideas and shared experiences (Moreno, 1994, p. 352). Sociodrama participants represent generalized socio-political-cultural roles rather than specific individuals, in that sociodrama "focuses its attention upon the collective denominators and it is not interested in the individual differentials or the private problems which they produce" (see footnote in Moreno, 1994, p. 364). Within a safe and structured sociodrama setting, individuals can gain a deeper understanding of the complexities of socio-political-cultural dynamics and their impact on the larger social organism, thereby contributing to Moreno's goal of promoting individual and collective well-being through increased awareness and empathy (see Kellermann, 2007b). Taken together, sociometry and sociodrama provide practical methods for studying, experiencing, and transforming social systems to promote concord, cohesion, and collective well-being.

---

[9] Also called "social psychodrama," mainly in Brazil. See Fleury et al., 2022.

3.4 Act Hunger, Action Insight, and Act Fulfillment

Moreno encouraged his protagonists to actively address their issues rather than rely solely on passive verbal communication. A core tenet of Morenian theory asserts that much like an infant's preverbal expression through action, the human desire to act emerges before the need for verbal expression (Moreno & Moreno, 1944). Accordingly, individuals are inclined to transcend the confines of verbal language to satisfy their *act hunger*, which is defined as a pronounced conscious or unconscious drive to express or experience that which has not been adequately satiated through embodied action. This innate hunger operates on what Moreno termed *open tension systems*; namely, intrapsychic or interpersonal issues that remain unresolved or unfulfilled (Garcia & Buchanan, 2009, p. 407). Protagonists often seek out psychodrama as a means to achieve *act fulfillment*; in other words, the completion of actions left incomplete and unresolved in their actual lives. This can often include fulfilling a need to say goodbye, expressing unspoken words or feelings, or resolving unfinished business. The concept of act hunger implies acknowledging that humans have a positive need for healing by embodying the fullness of an act (Blatner, 2000a, pp. 104, 113). The emphasis is placed on *action insight*, where a deeper understanding of the roots of an issue can be gained through deep and active experiential exploration (Kellermann, 2000a). Thus, in psychodrama, the participants are often fully immersed in the enacted scene to such an extent that they experience a state of flow (Csikszentmihalyi, 1991; Kipper, 1986, p. 59). Taken together, the sequence of act hunger, action insight, and act fulfillment represents a transformative psychotherapeutic process. Act hunger reflects the protagonist's need to express unresolved emotions or conflicts through action. This often leads to action insight, where a deeper awareness of behaviors and relationships emerges experientially. Finally, act fulfillment provides emotional resolution, integration, and a sense of closure, empowering protagonists to move forward with greater understanding and self-awareness.

3.5 Catharsis of Abreaction and Integration

Moreno took the concept of "catharsis" from Aristotle's *Poetics*, where it refers to the purging of pity and fear in the spectators of a Greek tragedy (Aristotle & Butcher, 1961), which Moreno termed "passive catharsis" (Moreno, 1994). In psychodrama, Moreno shifted the focus of catharsis from the audience to the stage by introducing active catharsis experienced by the protagonist and the supporting actors on stage (auxiliary egos). This active catharsis, termed *catharsis of abreaction*, involves discharging blocked and repressed emotions and thoughts. However, psychodramatists should avoid "pushing" the protagonist towards a cathartic experience (Nolte, 2020), since a peak experience of action insight or act fulfillment may sufficiently address the protagonist's psychological needs.

"Every catharsis of abreaction should be followed by a *catharsis of integration*" (Blatner, 1996, p. 64. emphasis added). Put simply, after releasing and becoming aware of previously disowned and repressed feelings, thoughts, and memories, the protagonist is supported to reclaim and reintegrate these aspects of the self constructively. This process involves re-owning repressed content and reintegrating split-off parts. Engaging in behavioral practices through role training, group sharing, and supportive closure aids in the integration process by (a) fostering a sense of mastery over the issue, (b) receiving support from the group, and (c) preparing individuals to face real-world challenges with renewed confidence (Blatner, 1996, p. 95).

4 Psychodrama Practice: An Overview

This section begins with an overview of the five basic elements of psychodrama and is followed by a description of the structure of what is commonly known as classical psychodrama. Next, core psychodramatic techniques are discussed, along with their position on the continuum of Moreno's developmental theory. This section concludes with a discussion of how Morenian psychodrama intersects with positive psychology, followed by my positive psychodrama program, comprising ten empirically supported activities that have been shown to foster personal growth and well-being.

4.1 The Five Basic Elements

Moreno named five fundamental elements of psychodrama, each briefly outlined below. Originally, the *stage* in psychodrama was raised and had a designated audience seating area and a balcony, where the latter symbolized transcendental concepts. In contrast, modern psychodramatists often work in standard rooms or studios, where a specific area is designated as the stage, with participants seated in a semi-circle around it. The *protagonist* is the person who is the focus of the psychodrama session and has chosen to explore a particular issue or situation. Protagonists use the stage to enact scenes from their lives, both past and present, and sometimes imagined future scenarios. Through this process, they gain new insights into their feelings, thoughts, and behaviors, and they can experiment with new ways of acting and reacting. The *auxiliary ego* is any group member who plays a role in the protagonist's psychodrama. They can play the part of a significant other, a symbolic figure, or even an abstract concept in psychodrama.

The *group* is made up of all the participants in the psychodrama session. They have a crucial role in the therapeutic process in that they provide a supportive and nonjudgmental environment for the protagonist. Group members participate in the sharing phase of the session, where they discuss their personal feelings and reactions to the enactment. However, they are not only spectators of the psychodrama, since group members can also take on the roles of auxiliary egos. Finally, the *psychodramatist* is the trained therapist who directs the psychodrama session by helping the protagonist choose an issue to explore and facilitating the therapeutic process by using psychodrama techniques. The psychodramatist ensures that the session is conducted safely, adheres to ethical standards and best practices, and guides the group through the sharing phase.

According to Kellermann (2000b),[10] the psychodramatist fulfills four key roles: *therapist*, by serving as the agent of change who ensures the therapeutic value of psychodrama through verbal and nonverbal interventions; *analyst*, by interpreting and giving meaning to the psychological dynamics and themes of the protagonist; *producer*, by staging the aesthetic experience through scenes and dramatic processes guided by therapeutic goals to facilitate change; and *group leader*, by managing group dynamics and fostering cohesion and trust within the group. Together, these somewhat overlapping roles support meaningful therapeutic and group processes in psychodrama, that help the protagonist and the group integrate their insights and experiences from the session into their everyday lives. It is important to note that in psychodrama aesthetic goals are always secondary to therapeutic goals, since the focus is on treatment rather than entertainment.

4.2 Session Structure

A classical psychodrama session typically follows a structured format that consists of three sequential phases: warm-up, action, and sharing (Blatner, 2000a). The *warm-up phase* – grounded in the precondition of a safe, nonjudgmental, and cohesive interpersonal setting – aims to foster participants' spontaneity, playfulness, engagement, and openness to exploration. The warm-up can be facilitated by a wide range of activities, including free conversation that expresses individual and group themes, theater games, and structured exercises that prepare the participants for a specific topic, such as the inner child, sibling relationships, family rules, body image, and so on (see for example Dayton, 1990, 2005).

---

[10] Kellermann (2000b) expanded Moreno's original three roles of the psychodramatist (therapist, analyst, and producer) by introducing the fourth role of a group leader.

The *action phase* constitutes the main segment of the session. The group typically designates one member (the protagonist) to be the focus of the session, but the action phase can also concentrate on interpersonal issues that preoccupy the group by using sociometric activities (Dayton, 2005). The specificity of psychodrama lies in encouraging protagonists to express their feelings in the first person in the here-and-now. The protagonists are directed to *show* rather than *tell*, and to *speak directly to* rather than *about* significant others in their lives, who are usually played by a group member (the auxiliary ego) or represented by an empty chair, thus allowing protagonists to *actively explore* their issues through the psychodramatic techniques.

One of the guiding frameworks for psychodrama direction is known as the *Psychodramatic Spiral* (Goldman & Morrison, 1984), which outlines a typical classical psychodrama session with a progression of scenes across time dimensions, from the periphery to the core issues. The session starts with a brief interview where the psychodramatist clarifies the presenting problem with the protagonist. Then, the protagonist chooses auxiliaries, and the psychodrama unfolds from the presentation of the problem in the present to the recent past. Next, as scenes unfold, the protagonist's *unmet psychological need*[11] and its related *act hunger* are identified. The psychodrama then progresses to deeper past experiences, often delving into childhood scenes. These often target *act fulfillment* and may or may not involve a cathartic peak. This process is followed by a "spiral back" toward the initial presenting problem with a concrete integration of insights gained during the preceding process (e.g., accepting the realization that parents did their best to provide for the family). Finally, role training for the future may involve actively embodying and experimenting with different roles, perspectives, and responses to enhance adaptability, problem-solving abilities, and interpersonal skills. The aim of this "rehearsal for life" is to prepare the protagonists to effectively navigate real-life challenges and future scenarios in their lives. The final moments on stage should facilitate adequate closure. As Giacomucci (2021) indicated: "There are multiple layers of closure in the process, including an aesthetically pleasing closure to the scene, emotional closure for the protagonist, closure for the role players, closure for the group, and closure for the psychodrama director and any other team members" (p. 270). As part of the closure, auxiliaries are instructed to *de-role* from the

---

[11] *Unmet psychological needs* refer to core emotional and relational needs that were not adequately fulfilled, often during early developmental stages or in significant relationships. Psychodrama aims to identify, process, and address these needs to cultivate change. Needs include, for example, safety and security, emotional expression, validation and acceptance, autonomy, competence and achievement, belonging, mutuality and reciprocity, as well as respect and recognition.

roles they played on stage as they depart the psychodramatic surplus reality and transition back to actual reality in the here-and-now. The Psychodramatic Spiral model visually mirrors Moreno's initial stage design. It illustrates the psychodrama process as it transitions from the periphery to the core and returns to the opening issue with new insights, thus closing the circle.

In the final *sharing phase*, all the participants are invited to engage in introspection and disclose candidly and subjectively with the group whether and how they related to the preceding psychodramatic work. They are instructed to speak from their own experience, using the first person, and to avoid offering analysis, criticism, opinions, advice, or interpretations of the protagonist's work (Ruscombe-King, 1998). The sharing phase, also known as the integration phase, reintegrates all the participants into the group and actual reality, by creating a space to share "our common humanity" (Z. T. Moreno, 2006, p. 234), similar to Yalom's concept of universality (Yalom & Leszcz, 2005). In this phase, those who have played a role in the psychodrama as auxiliaries may also be invited to share "role feedback" by giving constructive feedback on how they experienced the role they played (e.g., "As your mother, I felt proud/sorry that . . .").

It is also worth mentioning *The Hollander Psychodrama Curve*, another framework that visually outlines the progression of the intensity of the protagonist's emotional engagement and expression during a psychodrama session as a bell-shaped curve (Hollander, 2002). The vertical axis (Y) represents the emotional intensity continuum, while the horizontal axis (X) depicts the tripartite temporal continuum that progresses from warm-up through action to the sharing and integration phases. As the session progresses from the warm-up to the action phase, the protagonist's emotional intensity peaks, which involves deep emotional expression and catharsis. After the emotional climax, the curve shows a gradual decline in intensity as the session moves toward the sharing and integration phases. It is important to note that individuals progress through a psychodrama session at varying rates, and psychodramatists should adapt to their individual protagonists' unique needs without pressuring them toward a cathartic peak.

4.3 Core Techniques

A wide range of psychodrama techniques can be used during the action phase (Cruz et al., 2018; Z. T. Moreno, 1965). Moreno highlighted four core techniques that are situated along the continuum of his developmental theory (soliloquy, doubling, mirroring, and role reversal) that represent a growing recognition of and interaction with other individuals. The *soliloquy* technique involves having the protagonists voice (externalize) their inner dialogue, thoughts, and feelings as though they were speaking to themselves or engaging in an internal conversation. This technique fuels spontaneity and enhances self-clarity with respect to unmet psychological needs and their related act-hunger. From a developmental perspective, because the soliloquy technique only involves the protagonist, it coincides with the egocentric state in the first developmental phase, where infants perceive themselves as the entire universe and as undifferentiated from it. Unlike the soliloquy technique, the next three techniques are enacted with the help of the psychodramatist or auxiliary egos.

The *doubling* technique involves the psychodramatist or a group member articulating a feeling, thought, sensation, or other experience that the protagonist is unable to express. As Dayton (2016) noted, "the doubling can help protagonists bring to consciousness what may be swimming around inside of them in a semiconscious state" (p. 44). Doubling is performed not only verbally and vocally but also through gestures and body movements to emphasize a physical reaction or illustrate an abstract inner experience more concretely (Moreno, 2013). Occasionally, two or more doubles can be invited on stage to portray conflicting or complementing roles that the protagonist may play in life. An auxiliary ego can be invited to undertake the role of a *constant double* that doubles the protagonist throughout the entire psychodrama. Alternatively, a group member of the audience with something to contribute to the protagonist may ask to play the role of a *spontaneous double*. Offering the protagonist a spontaneous double engages the audience in relation to the psychodrama on stage. After the double has performed, it is crucial to ask the protagonist to either confirm the double and repeat it, correct or refine the double, and act on the corrected version, or reject it altogether. From a developmental perspective, because the doubling technique only involves the protagonist and another person who plays a "psychological twin," it coincides with the second developmental phase where the mother is naturally the infant's first auxiliary ego (Moreno & Moreno, 1944), which infants perceive as an extension of themselves (similar to Kohut's "self-object").[12] Zerka Moreno stated that a child needs self-affirmation before integrating into the world, "to be assured that being himself [*sic*] is a positive category" (Moreno, 2006, p. 193). Thus, parents should practice "affirmative doubling," starting when the child begins making sounds, by mirroring their baby or pre-verbal language.

Next, the *mirroring* technique involves the protagonist observing the psychodrama from the audience as the auxiliaries enact the scene. The mirroring technique is often used to cool down the protagonist by creating emotional

---

[12] Heinz Kohut (1913–1981), the founder of Self Psychology, introduced the concept of "self-object" to describe how parents or caregivers function as extensions of the self and contribute to its development.

distance through *aesthetic distance*: "the midpoint between cognitive detachment and emotional over-engagement, allowing individuals to simultaneously think about and feel their experiences" (Ben-Tzur & Feniger-Schaal, 2025, p. 1). Seeing themselves portrayed by others can prompt protagonists to engage more comfortably on stage (Kellermann, 2007a). The mirroring technique is useful when protagonists resist role-play, need to take on the role of the director to gain a sense of autonomy, and seek to understand how others perceive them. From a developmental perspective, because the mirroring technique involves protagonists observing their own reflection from the audience, played back from outside of the psychodramatic surplus reality, it also coincides with Moreno's second developmental phase of partial differentiation. As Bannister (2007) noted, infants begin to form their identity by experiencing their own feelings mirrored by caring parental figures. This identity is shaped and reflected back to them by those closest to them, which helps infants recognize their separateness from others.

Finally, the *role-reversal* technique involves having the protagonist take on the role of an absent person or different parts of themselves in the psychodrama. This technique concretizes Moreno's idea of the existential encounter in that it enables the protagonists not only to step into the role of another person and experience the situation and relationship through their perspective but also to gain insights into how the other person is experiencing them. Role reversal also helps clarify the state of other characters in the psychodrama, thus providing the protagonists with an opportunity to show their psychological state and behavior in the scene. Developmentally, because role reversal involves the realization that others exist as separate subjective beings, this technique coincides with the third developmental phase where there is a differentiation between self and other and between fantasy and reality (Kellermann, 2007a). Zerka Moreno noted that "the child is not able to role reverse with others until he [*sic*] recognizes his separateness. He cannot yield what he does not know. Lack of ability to role reverse indicates deep lack of early self-affirmation" (Moreno et al., 2006).

In addition to the four core techniques above, four other psychodrama techniques are frequently used. The *time regression* technique enables protagonists to re-experience a past event closest to the root of their problem: namely, to the *locus nascendi*, *status nascendi*, and *matrix* (Moreno, 1994). Focusing on a positive past event can increase the protagonist's motivation for change and ultimately generate a sense of competence (Orkibi, 2019). Psychodrama also explores future situations by applying the *future projection* technique that enables protagonists to explore their future self in the here-and-now, instead of only visualizing or talking about it. Protagonists explore and clarify expectations, goals, plans, and possibilities, as well as gain more hope, motivation, and confidence through preparation, rehearsal, and behavioral practice (Yablonsky, 1954). In the *empty chair* technique, the protagonist uses an empty chair to explore and express emotions, thoughts, and conflicts related to an absent person, situation, or parts of oneself situated on that chair. This technique is particularly useful in individual psychodrama, where there are no auxiliaries (e.g., Knittel, 2009).[13] Finally, the *psychodramatic image* (or *sculpting*) technique focuses on visual representation when the protagonist arranges auxiliaries in specific positions to symbolically portray aspects of their inner world, relationships, or emotional experiences (e.g., their relationship with their symptoms). The protagonist creates ("sculpts") the image from the outside, with another person or object representing them within the image if needed. The image can be either static, displaying a still representation, or dynamic, highlighting the interactions between its components. By engaging with the image both as an active participant on stage and as an observer from the audience's perspective, protagonists gain valuable insights into emotions, perceptions, and relational dynamics (Kushnir & Orkibi, 2021).

4.4 A Positive Psychodrama Program

There has been a surge in positive psychology interventions, which are defined as purposeful activities to cultivate positive emotions, behaviors, or thoughts (Sin & Lyubomirsky, 2009). These interventions are increasingly seen as valuable in their own right, and not only as supplements to traditional treatments. Mounting meta-analytic evidence suggests they significantly enhance well-being and resilience (Carr et al., 2021; Carr et al., 2024). Positive psychology interventions are further supported by the empirically based *Sustainable Happiness Model*, which suggests that approximately 40 percent of individuals' happiness can be influenced by their intentional activities, whereas genetics and circumstances contribute about 50 percent and 10 percent, respectively (Lyubomirsky et al., 2005). This model underscores the notion that through considerable intrinsic motivation and effort, intentional behavior can make a difference in one's well-being and optimal functioning (Sheldon & Lyubomirsky, 2021), thereby providing another rationale for offering positive psychodrama intervention programs. However, most positive psychology interventions rely heavily on written or talk-based methods, which have been criticized for being insufficiently "memorable or evocative to counter negative cognitive-affective content or generate enduring positivity" (Pugh & Salter, 2021, p. 4). This underscores the need for multisensory, experiential

---

[13] Moreno's empty chair technique has been integrated into various approaches, including Gestalt therapy and emotion-focused therapy.

methods such as positive psychodrama, that integrate emotional, cognitive, and bodily experiences into the therapeutic process.

Positive psychodrama is based on the premises (a) that "health is a state of complete physical, mental and social well-being and not merely the absence of disease or infirmity" (World Health Organization, 1948), and that (b) individuals without mental illness do not necessarily experience mental health; they may be languishing rather than thriving, where the former refers to a state of emptiness and stagnation, and the latter to optimal psychosocial well-being and fulfilling engagement with life (Keyes, 2002, 2013).

With respect to theory, both positive psychology (DeRobertis & Bland, 2021) and psychodrama are associated with the humanistic school of thought, which posits "that individuals are, at their core, searching for ways to improve their current functioning and maximize their potentialities" (Forsyth, 2015, p. 429). Accordingly, humans have the innate potential to change and improve their lives by tapping into their inner resources, fostering self-awareness, and making conscious choices aligned with their values and aspirations. This is consistent with the view that the psychodramatist's main role is to remove barriers to help protagonists awaken their own internal "autonomous healing center" – that is, individuals' innate capacity to heal themselves (Moreno, 2012, p. 504). Giacomucci (2021) further suggested that "psychodrama leverages the mutual aid between group members, effectively helping the group-as-a-whole to access its autonomous healing center" (p. 115).

In practical terms, *positive psychodrama* applies empirically supported positive psychology interventions through action-based practice to prioritize experiential applications over verbal communication. Positive psychodrama operates in multi-temporal dimensions where protagonists can re-enact events in the past, gain a broader perspective and awareness in the present, and explore possibilities or rehearse for anticipated events in the future (Orkibi, 2014, 2019, 2023b). Evidence suggests that positive psychology interventions incorporating diverse activities are more effective not only in combating boredom but also in addressing *hedonic adaptation* – the psychological tendency for individuals to return to a baseline level of happiness after experiencing positive or negative events (Neumeier et al., 2017). The positive psychodrama program presented below incorporates the following 10 activities, which positive psychology research has identified as essential for personal growth and well-being. The program outline is as follows:

1. Opening session
2. Character strengths

3. Self-compassion
4. Supportive relationships (social atom)
5. Active-constructive response
6. Gratitude (expressing)
7. Gratitude (receiving)
8. Forgiveness as self-care
9. Coping modes identification (6-part story and BASICPh)
10. Optimism (positive explanatory style)
11. Hope (goal, agency and pathway thinking)
12. Closing session

As seen, the program includes two additional sessions. An opening session (#1) is designed to facilitate participant introductions, foster cohesion, and familiarize them with the setting. A closing session (#12) is dedicated to farewells, reflection, summarizing the process, and evaluating participants' progress and achievements. The ideal session duration is three hours, with an optimal group size of 8 to 10 adult participants. However, these activities can also be applied in individual one-to-one sessions and even in organizations (Orkibi, 2023b).

Character strengths in positive psychology are the twenty-four trait-like capacities universally recognized as morally valuable that serve as concrete pathways for expressing corresponding virtues (Peterson & Seligman, 2004). For example, the interpersonal virtue of Humanity can be achieved through related character strengths such as kindness, love, and social intelligence. Intervention research has shown that helping clients to identify and then use their signature (i.e., top) character strengths can increase health and well-being (Pang & Ruch, 2019). Through psychodramatic role-play, participants explore, embody, and amplify their strengths, which, in turn, reinforce their unique virtues and capabilities (Peterson & Seligman, 2004). Specifically, the time regression technique can be used to enable protagonists to revisit a positive past situation when they demonstrated a character strength. Revisiting this scene helps protagonists reconnect with the emotions, thoughts, and actions tied to their strength, thereby enhancing self-awareness and empowerment. The protagonist may construct and explore a symbolic psychodramatic image of the strength or role-reverse with an empty chair representing a strength. The latter approach allows the psychodramatist to interview the protagonist (now in the seat of the strength) to explore its psycho-developmental origins, roles in the protagonist's life, and the factors that support its expression (Pugh & Salter, 2021). Alternatively, protagonists can describe their strength from the viewpoint of a significant person in their life, represented by another chair. This "external perspective" often helps articulate the protagonist's character strength and testifies to its effective application in the past. The multilingual VIA Survey of Character Strengths can be administered online to identify participants' unique character strengths profile, which identifies the top and bottom strengths out of twenty-four (https://www.viacharacter.org/).

Self-compassion is conceptualized as a bipolar continuum ranging from uncompassionate self-responding to compassionate self-responding in moments of distress (Neff, 2023). Based on Neff's (2023) self-compassion model, the psychodramatist encourages three processes that involve six elements: replacing *self-judgment* with *self-kindness*, which involves treating oneself with warmth and understanding rather than harsh self-criticism, self-blame, and shame; replacing a sense of *isolation* with the perception of *common humanity* by recognizing that suffering and imperfection are part of the human experience, which fosters a sense of connection with others rather than feeling isolated and ashamed; and replacing *overidentification* with *mindfulness*, which entails maintaining a balanced awareness of one's thoughts and emotions without becoming overwhelmed or overly identified with them. With this in mind, and drawing on compassion-focused therapy chairwork, the psychodramatic activity facilitates a dialogue between three parts of the self: the self-critic, the criticized self, and the compassionate self (Bell et al., 2020). The protagonist first embodies the self-critic role and expresses criticism toward the empty chair, then moves to the opposite chair to "receive," embody, and verbalize this experience. After repeating this process as needed, the protagonist transitions to a third chair to reflect on the interaction and embody the "compassionate self." From this role, the protagonist responds to both the "critic" and "criticized" parts of the self with compassion by focusing on the fears and unmet needs underlying the critic rather than suppressing or prematurely soothing away these conflicting self-parts. The compassionate self gradually fosters a voice of self-kindness, acknowledges shared humanity, and establishes healthy boundaries. To deepen this experience, the psychodramatist can introduce sensory aids, such as a soft blanket, to concretize the kind and nurturing qualities of self-compassion (Lawrence, 2015). The 18-item State Self-Compassion Scale assesses the six components of self-compassion, and a 6-item short form assesses overall state self-compassion (Neff et al., 2021).

In the social realm, *supportive relationships* are identified in one's social atom map, a visual representation of an individual's social network (Buchanan, 1984). The action sociogram, the dramatization of a social atom in action, can further explore and shed light on the impact of these positive relationships on the protagonist's life. Social support refers to the social resources that individuals perceive to be available (perceived social support) or that are actually provided to them by others (actual or received social support) to help them cope with life stressors (Cohen et al., 2000). Studies have shown that one's belief in the availability of social support is more critical to well-being than actual received social support (Chu et al., 2010; Cohen & Wills, 1985). Perceived social support has been positively and causally associated with mental health, physical health, longevity, and subjective well-being (Orkibi & Ronen, 2015; Thoits, 2011; Uchino et al., 2012).

Another interpersonal activity focuses on learning the most positive way to respond to someone's good news; namely, by reacting with an *active-constructive response* that expresses genuine interest, excitement, and enthusiasm (Gable et al., 2004). This is achieved by asking questions to elicit additional details about the positive event and emphasizing the possible benefits of the event and its meaningfulness for the sharer, which enhances trust, closeness, and satisfaction in interpersonal relationships (Gable & Reis, 2010; Lambert et al., 2013). The active-constructive response contrasts with the passive-constructive response (when the responder does not say much or is quiet about the positive event), the passive-destructive response (when the responder changes the topic, minimally acknowledges or totally ignores the event shared), or the active-destructive response (when the responder is involved but focuses on the negative implications of the event or minimizes its significance to the sharer). In positive psychodrama, the role-play of past (but also fictional) scenarios can help protagonists recognize their response patterns and adopt an active-constructive response. Consistent with Moreno's role theory, each response pattern is conceptualized as a distinct role, such as the "active-constructive *responder*." The 12-item Perceived Responses to Capitalization Attempts scale measures a general tendency toward one of the response types and can be used to identify responses in specific situations (Gable et al., 2004).

Gratitude is cultivated through reflection and expression of appreciation for life's blessings, and has been shown to support emotional and social well-being (Jans-Beken et al., 2020). In positive psychodrama, protagonists role-play encounters in which they express and receive gratitude to or from a person represented by an empty chair or an auxiliary ego. In the *expressing gratitude* activity, group members are invited to write a detailed gratitude letter to a living person who has done something good and meaningful for them and to whom they are grateful but have never thanked. They are instructed to write as though addressing this person directly ("Dear David"), describe in specific terms what this person did, why they are grateful to this person, and how this person's deed affected their life, as concretely as possible (Emmons, 2013). The chosen protagonist is then invited to participate in a "virtual" gratitude visit using role-play with the benefactor represented by an empty chair (Tomasulo, 2019), and read the letter to that person. The protagonist can also reverse the role to become the benefactor and respond. Finally, the protagonist is encouraged to deliver the gratitude letter to the actual benefactor within a week. In the *receiving gratitude* activity, protagonists identify someone who appreciates their existence or a past deed, thereby allowing them to experience receiving gratitude from others. Pugh and Salter (2021) propose prompting the appreciative other, played by the protagonist, to reflect on how they would respond if their positive feedback were dismissed by the protagonist as a way to address the human tendency to downplay positive qualities. For example, the psychodramatist can say: "Dan, you may know that Cathy [the protagonist] often discounts her positive qualities. What would you say to her about that? How would you like her to receive and acknowledge the gratitude you've expressed?" To measure changes in gratitude, researchers and practitioners can utilize the 20-item self-report State Gratitude Scale (Spence et al., 2014).

Another interpersonal construct is *forgiveness*, which has been shown to promote positive changes in various psychological health outcomes (Rasmussen et al., 2019). In positive psychodrama, forgiveness work first permits the offended person to actualize their act-hunger to fully express negative thoughts, feelings, and motives directly to the wrongdoer, who is represented by an empty chair (but is not present). Then, the psychodramatist uses the doubling technique to validate the experience of the offended person who describes not only the consequences of the wrongdoing but also the consequences of their own unforgiveness in terms of its associated negative ("toxic") emotions, thoughts, and motives. Reasons for not forgiving the wrongdoer are also explored (e.g., wanting to take revenge). Acknowledging the negative impact of unforgiveness on the offended person helps clients make an intentional decision to forgive the wrongdoer and let go of the past – a process often called "decisional forgiveness" (Worthington et al., 2007). The aim is to decrease or neutralize the offended person's negativity associated with unforgiveness and evoke neutral emotions (i.e., that do not have a positive or negative valence) toward the wrongdoer and the wrongdoing. Forgiveness is thus an intentional act of self-care, self-empowerment, and self-liberation from pain and suffering. Sometimes, replacing negative thoughts and emotions with positive ones may also be an option, depending on the nature of the wrongdoing and the offended person's willingness and readiness to do so, in a process often called "emotional forgiveness" (Worthington et al., 2007). When appropriate, the role-reversal technique may enable the offended person to step into the wrongdoer's shoes and gain insights into that person's viewpoint about the wrongdoing. This, in turn, may evoke other-oriented positive emotions in the offended person, such as empathy, sympathy, and even compassion. Changes in forgiveness can be measured on the 15-item Forgiveness Scale that assesses forgiveness toward a specific wrongdoer (Rye et al., 2001).

Participants' dominant *coping modes* can be identified and strengthened through the 6-Part Story activity, a projective method that aims to empower individuals to navigate stress and adversity through the identification of their adaptive coping modes (Lahad, 2017; Lahad et al., 2013). Clients are asked to write a story, based on the Hero's Journey structure, while responding to six questions: Who is the protagonist and the setting? What is the protagonist's mission? Who or what can be of assistance? Who or what obstacle prevents the protagonist from carrying out the mission? How does the protagonist cope with this obstacle? What happens next (i.e., how does the story end or continue)? The story is then analyzed to identify the protagonist's dominant coping modes using the BASICPh framework, which stands for *b*eliefs, *a*ffect, *s*ocial interactions, *i*magination, *c*ognition, and *ph*ysical coping modes (see Lahad et al., 2013).

Optimism has been operationalized based on people's *explanatory style*:[14] namely, their tendency to explain hypothetical scenarios and real-life events in a particular manner based on three dimensions: internality (internal vs. external cause, thus reflecting a level of personal responsibility), stability (permanent/stable/long-lasting vs. temporary/unstable), and globality (specific/local vs. generalized) (Buchanan & Seligman, 1995). A person with an optimistic explanatory style is likely to explain problems, setbacks, and failures as due to external, temporary, and specific causes and explain positive events as due to internal, permanent, and generalized causes. Conversely, a person with a pessimistic explanatory style is likely to explain problems as due to internal, permanent, and generalized causes and positive events as due to external, temporary, and specific causes (Smith et al., 2013). To foster a positive outlook on life's possibilities (Reivich et al., 2023) by developing an optimistic explanatory style, positive psychodrama invites protagonists to role-play hypothetical and real-world scenarios during which the doubling technique is used to explore inner thoughts in terms of the explanatory style. Maladaptive pessimistic thoughts are challenged with optimistic ones based on the internality, stability, and globality dimensions. The Attributional Style Questionnaire (Peterson, 1988) is a self-report tool that scores explanatory style on six positive and six negative hypothetical events that can be dramatized and explored using the doubling technique addressing the three causal dimensions. By adopting a broader approach to optimism interventions, protagonists can use psychodrama to explore what it might feel like to live in a more optimistic future within

---

[14] The term "attributional style" is often used interchangeably in the literature.

a specific context. This approach aligns with research suggesting that vividly imagining positive future events correlates with higher levels of optimism (Ji et al., 2017). The widely used 10-item revised Life Orientation Test (Scheier et al., 1994) can be administered to assess clients' changes in their general outlook on life.

Finally, according to Snyder (2000), *Hope*[15] is a tripartite motivational construct comprised of a valuable goal (short- or long-term), pathway thinking (i.e., a person's perceived ability to generate multiple workable paths to that goal, including pathways to overcome obstacles), and agency thinking (i.e., a person's perceived ability to utilize these paths to achieve the goal). Hope has been associated with psychological and physical well-being outcomes (Alarcon et al., 2013), including a sense of agency and purpose in people's lives (Murphy, 2023). In positive psychodrama, hope consists of finding the way and the will to achieve one's goals. The future projection technique enables protagonists to explore the experience of being their best possible future self in the here-and-now (Yablonsky, 1954), instead of only visualizing or writing about it. Snyder's (2002) 6-item State Hope scale can help measure changes in pathways and agency thinking as indicators of general hope. The Goal-Specific Hope scale measures hope regarding a particular goal (Feldman et al., 2009).

Overall, positive psychodrama is designed to cultivate these empirically supported constructs and provide an expressive-creative experience to enhance personal growth and well-being (Orkibi, 2014, 2019, 2023b). Future research is needed to examine the processes and outcomes of this positive psychodrama program.

5 Outcome Research: Does Psychodrama Work?

Academic publications on psychodrama have primarily focused on illustrative case studies or clinical vignettes. This tendency likely stems from the relative isolation of psychodrama from mainstream behavioral sciences. Unlike counselors, psychologists, and some creative arts therapists who are affiliated with research universities, many psychodramatists work in private clinics, which may limit their ability to conduct rigorous research, publish papers with hard evidence of efficacy, or train new generations of graduate students who can further develop theory and study the effectiveness of psychodrama.

Nevertheless, the evidence-based outcome findings provide valuable information on the effectiveness of psychodrama in real-world settings, which can inform clinical practice, policy decisions, and the development of evidence-based treatment. Recently, we conducted a systematic review and meta-analysis

---

[15] Hope and optimism are distinct yet related constructs. See Alarcon et al., 2013.

of thirty independent controlled studies on the effectiveness of drama-based therapies (i.e., psychodrama and drama therapy), reporting on 144 effect sizes and involving a total of 1,567 participants (Orkibi et al., 2023). We found a significant medium effect ($d = .501$, [.36, .64]) of drama-based therapies on mental health outcomes in clinical settings, schools, communities, and private practice. There was no statistically significant difference between psychodrama and drama therapy as treatment modalities.

5.1 Types of Outcome Research

Outcome research in psychotherapy focuses on evaluating the effectiveness of therapeutic interventions in achieving desired outcomes, such as symptom reduction, behavioral change, or improvement in overall well-being. Outcome studies typically involve measuring specific outcomes before and after an intervention is delivered. This allows researchers to determine whether the intervention significantly affected the targeted outcomes and whether any changes observed can be attributed to the intervention itself.

Various research designs can be utilized in outcome studies. The *randomized controlled trial* (RCT) design is considered the "gold standard" in research. It employs random assignment of participants to either an intervention group, a control group receiving no treatment, or a group with an active comparator, such as a different intervention or standard care (Nezu & Nezu, 2007). Randomization aims to ensure that each participant has an equal chance of being assigned to any group, thus minimizing selection bias, ensuring group comparability at the outset, and reducing the risk of confounding variables. This enables researchers to confidently attribute any observed differences between groups to the intervention itself.

In pharmacological research, RCTs often use blinding procedures to minimize selection bias. The blinding of participants and staff (who do not know whether they are receiving or delivering the treatment or the placebo) aims to prevent their expectations or motivations from directly or indirectly influencing study outcomes. However, unlike pharmacological research, this bias is impossible to avoid in psychotherapy research since therapists know what treatment they are delivering, and clients are not only aware of receiving that treatment but also have expectations concerning the treatment (Munder & Barth, 2018). For this reason, psychotherapy researchers aim to reduce selection bias by the: (a) use of an active control group with a credible treatment involving comparable treatment expectancies, and (b) assessment of client-perceived "treatment expectancies or credibility prior to or early (i.e., after the first session) in treatment and in which the treatment group had equal (zero difference) or lower expectancies or credibility than the control group received" (Laird et al., 2017, Appendix C, p. 4). Well-designed RCTs with a sufficiently large sample size ensure adequate statistical power to identify significant differences in outcomes between the groups being compared (e.g., treatment vs. control). Furthermore, a large sample size with diverse participant populations can yield findings that are more generalizable to broader populations, thereby enhancing the external validity of the results and increasing confidence in the intervention's applicability to real-world settings. Thus, an adequate sample size, combined with rigorous statistical analyses, enhances the reliability and robustness of the findings.

There are *three main approaches to RCTs*. It has been argued that "most RCTs aim to determine whether one intervention is superior to another" (Piaggio et al., 2012, p. 2594); hence, these are termed *superiority trials*. In contrast, a *noninferiority trial* aims to demonstrate that an intervention (often a new one) is not clinically worse than the standard (or other) treatment by more than a predefined margin of noninferiority (Piaggio et al., 2012). Noninferiority trials are typically conducted when demonstrating superiority over an existing treatment is not feasible, such as when the standard treatment is well-established or when the new intervention offers other advantages, such as greater availability, reduced cost, or greater ease of administration. The new treatment is recommended if it is similar to the standard treatment for a specified primary outcome. Any superiority of the new treatment in achieving the primary outcome would provide an additional advantage. However, because failure to show a difference does not mean treatments are equivalent, an *equivalence trial* aims to demonstrate that two treatments are considered therapeutically equivalent, indicating equal effectiveness within a predefined margin of equivalence (Piaggio et al., 2012). The objective is to establish both treatments as statistically and clinically equivalent without establishing one as superior. Equivalence trials assess interchangeability between treatments, particularly when demonstrating superiority is not the primary goal.

Psychodrama researchers are urged to use the CONSORT (Consolidated Standards of Reporting Trials) Statement, which includes a checklist and a flow diagram, as a guideline designed to assist authors in enhancing the reporting quality of findings derived from RCTs (Butcher et al., 2022; Schulz et al., 2010). There is also an extension to the main Statement that specifies guidelines for reporting noninferiority and equivalence randomized trials (Piaggio et al., 2012). For reporting RCTs with a parallel-group design with three or more groups, see Juszczak et al. (2019). Reporting guidelines for various designs can be searched at https://www.equator-network.org/.

Conducting a large-scale RCT may not always be feasible for ethical, practical, or logistical reasons (Baker, 2022). Ethically, it may be considered unacceptable to withhold potentially beneficial treatment from participants in the control group, particularly when substantial evidence supports its effectiveness. Resource constraints, including financial limitations and inadequate research infrastructure, can pose significant practical challenges to conducting RCTs. In addition, recruiting and retaining sufficient participants can be challenging since long-term follow-up periods and participant attrition further complicate RCT implementation. Logistical challenges such as coordinating multi-site studies, ensuring compliance with regulatory requirements, and addressing cultural considerations may also hinder RCT feasibility (Baker, 2022).

Controlled clinical trials (CCTs) can be applied when RCTs are not feasible. CCTs implement a quasi-experimental design resembling experimental studies but lack random assignment to treatment or control groups. In quasi-experimental studies, researchers compare groups that already exist naturally or are formed based on specific criteria (e.g., age, gender, severity of condition) rather than randomly assigning participants to groups. While such quasi-experimental studies allow researchers to investigate the effects of an intervention or treatment in real-world settings, they are more susceptible to bias and confounding variables than RCTs. CCTs typically include nonequivalent groups that may differ on various characteristics due to the lack of randomization. In studies employing a nonrandomized group comparison design, matching or assessing pretest equivalence can enhance confidence in attributing observed differences between groups at posttest to the treatment rather than to any preexisting differences. Examples include two psychodrama studies featuring a control group of participants matched on several factors to mitigate potential pre-treatment differences that might introduce selection bias (Gatta et al., 2010; Oguzhanoglu et al., 2013). Despite this limitation, quasi-experimental studies are valuable for evaluating interventions when randomization is not feasible or ethical (Orkibi et al., 2017). Psychodrama researchers designing a CCT are encouraged to adhere to the Transparent Reporting of Evaluations with Nonrandomized Designs (TREND) guidelines (Jarlais et al., 2004).

Psychodrama researchers may choose to utilize a *single-case experimental design* (SCED) when a control group is unavailable or unfeasible. This design evaluates the effects of an intervention on a single individual or a small group of individuals, with repeated measures of the outcome variables collected over time. Compared to a single group pretest-posttest design (discussed below), SCED provides more certainty on whether the intervention is responsible for change because it involves multiple measures throughout the treatment, where individual clients serve as their own control for comparison purposes (Kazdin, 2011). Therefore, SCED involves fewer study participants than studies with parallel group designs, such as RCTs and CCTs. Although underutilized in psychodrama research, SCED holds significant potential.

A classical SCED begins with a nontreatment baseline phase ("A") to establish a stable benchmark for the outcome variable scores, which is then compared to scores in the subsequent treatment phase and thus is crucial to the researcher's ability to interpret the effectiveness of the treatment. This is followed by the intervention phase ("B"), where the treatment under investigation is administered. The next phase involves a return to the nontreatment phase ("A"). Therefore, this design is often called a withdrawal or reversal design, denoted "ABA" (Morgan & Morgan, 2008).

SCED is widely employed in applied field studies. It can "provide a rigorous experimental evaluation of intervention effects ... [and] a strong basis for establishing causal inference" (Kratochwill et al., 2010, p. 2). SCED has strong internal validity due to the frequent data collection. Established standards for SCED require a minimum of three clients and five data points in a phase and at least three phases to meet evidence standards without reservations. For example, five systematic measures before (i.e., at baseline), during, and after the treatment ("ABA") may demonstrate an effect when the data pattern in the treatment phase differs from that observed in the baseline phase. Crucially, in applied real-world settings, the duration of a nontreatment phase may be limited by clinical and ethical constraints. Psychodrama researchers can benefit from consulting the single-case design technical documentation of the What Works Clearinghouse when designing SCED (Kratochwill et al., 2010). The Single-Case Reporting Guideline In BEhavioural Interventions (SCRIBE) should be used when writing about a SCED study for publication in a scientific journal (Tate et al., 2016).

In a *crossover design*, participants switch ("cross over") from one treatment sequence to another during the study (Lim & In, 2021). In a crossover study design, participants receive two or more treatments (e.g., psychodrama, art therapy) at different times. The sequence of treatments is randomized for each participant. The most straightforward design is the two-period, two-sequence crossover design (AB/BA design), where participants are randomly assigned to either the "AB" or "BA" sequence. Participants in the "AB" sequence initially receive treatment "A," followed by treatment "B," while those in the "BA" sequence receive treatment "B" first, followed by treatment "A." To eliminate the effects of the treatment in the first period in the second period ("carryover effect"), a "washout period" of nontreatment should be introduced between the periods (Dwan et al., 2019). However, if the washout period is excessively lengthy, it may lead to a higher dropout rate during the second period. Thus, the possible disadvantages of utilizing a crossover design include an extended trial duration, carryover effects, and participant dropout. Psychodrama researchers should thus use the adapted version of the 2010 CONSORT checklist for crossover designs, which incorporates a modified flowchart and baseline table to enhance reporting transparency (Dwan et al., 2019).

Finally, when a control group is unavailable and repeated measures are unfeasible, studies with a *single group pretest-posttest* design are sometimes the only viable option in applied research in natural field settings. This design is quasi-experimental, and some consider it uninterpretable given the multiple threats to internal validity associated with the lack of a control group (Heppner et al., 2015). Although this design allows the researcher to determine whether a change occurred between pretest and posttest, this change may be attributed to factors other than the treatment, such as history (i.e., an event that can impact the outcome) or maturation (i.e., clients' natural growth or development). Thus, studies with a single group pretest-posttest design have less certainty than a crossover design, RCT, CCT, and SCED.

5.2 Assessment of Potential Biases

Several types of biases should be considered when conducting rigorous RCTs and CCTs research in psychodrama (Orkibi & Feniger-Schaal, 2019). These include the following:

- *Selection bias*: occurs when there are systematic differences between the characteristics of participants in different study groups that could influence study outcomes. It can arise when participants are not randomly assigned to treatment groups, as in CCTs, or from poorly conducted randomization in RCTs. Standard methods of random sequence generation include computer-generated random numbers and random number tables. Relatedly, allocation concealment ensures the unbiased implementation of the randomization sequence, which prevents researchers from influencing group assignments and thus maintains randomization integrity.
- *Performance bias*: occurs when knowledge of the allocated interventions affects the participants, therapists, or researchers in ways that could influence study outcomes. This bias is unavoidable in psychotherapy research, since the stakeholders are aware of what type of therapy they are receiving or delivering (Munder & Barth, 2018).

- *Detection bias*: occurs when outcome assessors are not blind to treatment allocation or if there are differences in how outcomes are assessed between groups. Blinding outcome assessors and using objective outcome measures can help reduce detection bias (Munder & Barth, 2018).
- *Attrition bias*: occurs when there are systematic differences in the dropout rates or loss to follow-up between treatment groups, and the reasons for dropout are related to the outcomes being measured. If participants disproportionally drop out of the study from one treatment group, it can introduce bias into the results. Adequately addressing missing data and conducting intention-to-treat analyses can help mitigate attrition bias (Gupta, 2011).
- *Reporting bias*: occurs when study outcomes or analyses are selectively reported, leading to an incomplete or doctored representation of the study results. This bias can arise if researchers selectively report outcomes that show statistically significant results or fail to report nonsignificant or unfavorable outcomes. Transparent reporting of all pre-specified outcomes and adherence to reporting guidelines can help reduce reporting bias, such as the American Psychological Association's journal article reporting standards for quantitative research in psychology (Appelbaum et al., 2018).
- *Other biases*: This category includes any additional sources of bias specific to the study design or context that could affect the validity of the findings, such as funding bias, publication bias, or conflicts of interest. Identifying and addressing these potential biases is essential for accurately interpreting the study results and drawing valid conclusions.

When conducting rigorous research in psychodrama, it is of utmost importance to address these types of biases. They can significantly impact the results, thus underscoring the need for their mitigation. By doing so, researchers can enhance the credibility and robustness of their research outcomes and thus contribute to a more comprehensive understanding of the effectiveness of psychodrama interventions and, more generally, enhance the credibility of the field's evidence base.

5.3 Treatment Fidelity

Fidelity refers to how closely an intervention is implemented as intended, with adequate *adherence* to the manual and its theory-specified techniques or methods, including content, coverage, frequency, and duration (Carroll et al., 2007). Fidelity also refers to the *quality* (i.e., competence or skillfulness) with which these techniques or methods are implemented. Adherence and quality are both considered to reflect treatment integrity. Another component of implementation fidelity is *treatment differentiation*, which refers to the extent to which the treatment of interest differs from a comparison or control condition (Hildebrand et al., 2012). Variations in adherence and quality must be minimized, and treatment differentiation maximized to rigorously assess the effectiveness of a given treatment.

Two other components of implementation fidelity are noteworthy and focus on the participants (clients) rather than the provider (therapists). *Treatment receipt* assesses participants' comprehension of the treatment content, as intended by the providers, during its delivery (Bellg et al., 2004). Assessment methods can include self-reports, interviews, and observational ratings. *Treatment enactment* assesses the extent to which participants apply the "lessons learned" during the treatment (e.g., skills acquired, behaviors rehearsed, coping strategies, insights) in real-life situations (Bellg et al., 2004). Self-reports, interviews, and journaling can be used to monitor performance outside of the clinic.

Not assessing or monitoring treatment fidelity raises the risk of dismissing potentially beneficial interventions that may not have worked due to inadequate implementation, or endorsing ineffective interventions where desired outcomes were attained but were not due to the intervention itself. Accurate fidelity assessment is essential for drawing clear conclusions about intervention effectiveness (internal validity) and generalizability (external validity) (Ginsburg et al., 2021). Research has suggested that therapists' self-reports can be a practical method to assess basic counseling techniques, but found that discrepancies emerged between supervisor and therapist ratings of more complex techniques. Further, therapists, as compared to supervisors, overestimate their adherence to evidence-based interventions (Carroll et al., 2010). Thus, in addition to ongoing supervision and performance-based feedback, using video-recorded sessions or self-report implementation checklists can contribute to the ongoing assessment of fidelity (Ang et al., 2018). While fidelity assessment tools are specific to each intervention, their crucial role calls for their development and utilization in psychodrama interventions, similar to other therapies (e.g., Denton et al., 2009).

Ensuring fidelity is especially crucial in *complex interventions* with multiple interacting components (Ginsburg et al., 2021). There is evidence that simple and precisely defined interventions tend to be executed with greater implementation fidelity than those that are ambiguous and overly complex (Carroll et al., 2007). Less complex interventions also have higher levels of reliability in terms of inter-rater agreement in assessing treatment fidelity (Ginsburg et al., 2021). Thus, simplicity and clarity should be considered when designing an intervention to ensure greater implementation fidelity and consistency in practice.

5.4 Differentiating Psychodrama

Adhering to an intervention may not necessarily entail implementing every single component. Successful and meaningful implementations can still be achieved if only the intervention's "essential components" are implemented. This approach to treatment differentiation facilitates adapting an intervention to local needs (Carroll et al., 2007).

Because psychodrama is often not a manualized treatment, it is crucial to operationally pre-define the essential components of psychodrama treatment during the research design phase. Then, during treatment, competent adherence to this definition should be monitored. For example, the essential components can include (a) transitioning into the psychodramatic reality and enacting at least one scene that approximates a real-life situation or externalizes the protagonist's inner experience, (b) applying at least one of the four core psychodrama techniques (soliloquy, doubling, mirroring, role reversal), and (c) having group members play roles in the protagonist's enactment (Kellermann, 2000b, pp. 19–20; McVea et al., 2011, p. 418). In applied research, as long as the essential components of a treatment are competently adhered to, the treatment can be somewhat flexible and adaptable as a function of the protagonist's needs. To differentiate between psychodrama and drama therapy, researchers should consider both the therapist's qualifications and the intervention content and theoretical framework. While both operate within a dramatic (surplus) reality, in psychodrama, the story and characters are reality-based, whereas, in drama therapy, they are primarily fantasy-based, imaginary, and symbolic (Kedem-Tahar & Kellermann, 1996; Orkibi et al., 2023). Finally, because classical psychodrama is protagonist-centered, it is crucial to report the number of sessions for the entire group and clarify how many psychodramas each participant was engaged in as the protagonist. Because psychodrama interventions are often reported with insufficient details (Orkibi & Feniger-Schaal, 2019), researchers should use the TIDieR (Template for Intervention Description and Replication) checklist and guidelines which were developed to help improve completeness in the reporting of the treatment provided (Hoffmann et al., 2014). An example of applying the TIDieR can be found in the online supplementary materials for our RCT on tele-drama therapy for community-dwelling older adults with constricted life-space mobility (Elkarif et al., 2024).

5.5 Feasibility and Acceptability Studies

Pilot studies designed to examine feasibility and acceptability are often overlooked in psychodrama research. However, they are essential for evaluating interventions within specific settings or populations before conducting an intervention study, especially for RCTs and CCTs. *Feasibility* studies focus on logistical considerations such as the availability of resources, ease of implementation and data collection, cost-effectiveness, and any potential barriers or challenges that may arise. On the other hand, *acceptability* studies explore stakeholders' (clients, therapists, administrators) perceptions, attitudes, and satisfaction with the intervention by examining factors such as perceived usefulness, appropriateness, and satisfaction with the delivery of the intervention. These studies are essential in the preliminary phases of a research project because they help identify implementation issues, refine protocols, and tailor interventions to enhance successful uptake. Orsmond and Cohn (2015) offer valuable guidance for researchers in ways to formulate the key questions that are critical for studying feasibility and acceptability. The CONSORT Statement extension to randomized pilot and feasibility trials is also recommended to improve the transparency and quality of reporting the study (Eldridge et al., 2016).

6 Change Process Research: How Does Psychodrama Work?

Given the mounting evidence that psychodrama positively affects various health outcomes (Orkibi et al., 2023), it is essential to investigate the factors that contribute to these benefits. Recently, psychodrama and drama therapy researchers have expanded their inquiries from focusing solely on outcomes to examining therapeutic change factors, mechanisms (de Witte et al., 2021), and processes (Frydman et al., 2022). By implementing this line of research, psychodrama has effectively caught up with other psychotherapy approaches that initiated change process research years ago (Elliott, 2010; Gelo et al., 2015; Greenberg, 1986; Lambert, 2013a; Timulak, 2008).

Whereas psychotherapy outcome research inquires whether or not treatment leads to change, change process research inquires *how* psychotherapy leads to change (Kazdin, 2009). *Change process research* is defined as the study of "the content of psychological therapy sessions and the mechanisms through which client change is achieved, both in single sessions and across time" (Hardy & Llewelyn, 2015, p. 184). Hence, a change event, which can be considered an *immediate process outcome* or "small o" (e.g., action insight), is a component that builds the continuous change process and, in doing so, influences the final outcome, the "big O" (e.g., anxiety; Krause, 2024, p. 272).

Change process research is crucial to the advancement of psychodrama because it helps (a) identify specific therapeutic factors that can account for how therapeutic change occurs, (b) improve the effectiveness of psychodrama interventions, (c) refine a theory of change that provides a rationale and structure for psychodrama interventions, and (d) develop more effective training and supervision on therapeutic change factors that are supported by evidence (Hardy & Llewelyn, 2015).

Hardy and Llewelyn (2015) categorized process research into three progressive types. *Descriptive studies* provide accounts of behaviors and processes observed during therapy or in participants' beliefs, feelings, and behaviors without a theoretical base. *Hypothesis testing studies* attempt to predict outcomes based on variables hypothesized to be critical for the effectiveness of therapy. *Theory-building studies* examine how psychological change occurs, often without a single pathway to change, while viewing it as a multidimensional process that is also influenced by internal and external events. Research methods vary and include quantitative, qualitative, and mixed approaches. Relatedly, *process-outcome studies* examine the relationship between the process occurring during therapy and its outcomes and often aim to identify which specific process is the most effective in producing the desirable outcome (Crits-Christoph et al., 2013). For an example of a psychodrama process-outcome study, see Orkibi et al. (2017).

Data Sources and Types

Data in change process research can be collected from one or preferably several perspectives, since change can stem from the client, therapist, or relational processes (Elliott, 2012). For instance, the client-therapist therapeutic alliance can be measured by self-reports from both client and therapist (Horvath & Greenberg, 1989) and by an observational coding tool (McLeod & Weisz, 2005). The type of change can be cognitive, behavioral, emotional, physiological, and/or neurobiological, while the locus of change can be at the individual, interpersonal, and/or group levels. Change process research may probe the entire therapeutic process, an entire session, segments of sessions, significant in-session events, and a wide range of client-therapist interactions. Psychodrama researchers can benefit from adopting data collection methods utilized in other experiential therapies that have extensively investigated therapeutic change factors and processes (see Elliott et al., 2004a, 2004b; Elliott et al., 2013).

Change Process Research Questions

Hayes et al. (2008) proposed three key questions that process research can address:

- What is the *pattern* of change over the course of treatment (e.g., linear, quadratic, cubic, etc.)?
- How does change occur (*predictors* of change, *mediators*, and *mechanisms*)?

- What are the moderators of change (e.g., client or therapist characteristics, treatment dose, contextual or environmental factors, etc.)?

Other key questions that psychodrama researchers can probe include:

- How do clients in the roles of protagonists, auxiliaries, or audience members experience therapeutic change throughout the course of psychodrama group therapy?
- What specific psychodrama techniques contribute to protagonist change?
- What are the psychological, physiological, and neurological mechanisms underlying therapeutic change associated with a specific psychodrama technique?
- What roles do in-session therapeutic change factors (e.g., engagement, spontaneity, action insight, act fulfillment, catharsis) play in the change process?
- How do relational dynamics (e.g., psychodramatist-protagonist therapeutic alliance, synchronization) impact the effectiveness of psychodrama?

6.1 Common and Specific Therapeutic Factors

In pharmacological research, "active ingredients" refers to how a drug exerts an effect. I have opted for the term *therapeutic change factors* (or more simply, change factors) because it has been frequently used in the context of psychodrama (Kellermann, 1985), creative arts therapies (de Witte et al., 2021; Orkibi & Keisari, 2023), and psychotherapy (Huber et al., 2021; Krause, 2024; MacNair-Semands et al., 2010). Nevertheless, these terms are often used interchangeably in the literature (e.g., Kapitan, 2012). In essence, a therapeutic change factor is a single component that accounts for a therapeutic effect (Tarashoeva et al., 2022).

Common factors (also termed nonspecific or universal factors) are therapeutic change factors that are common to all psychotherapeutic approaches. Common factors are a-theoretical in that they are broad and not rooted in a specific theory of change but rather are related to client characteristics, therapist characteristics, and their interactions (Wampold, 2015). A table listing the foremost common factors in the general psychotherapy literature can be seen in a scoping review publication where my colleagues and I reviewed therapeutic factors across the creative arts therapies (de Witte et al., 2021). The most frequently researched common factor is the therapeutic alliance (i.e., client-therapist relationship), which has been argued to be the only common factor for which "it has been possible to perform meta-analyses that clearly demonstrate the impact of this factor on final outcomes" (Krause, 2024, p. 261).

Many comparative studies have reported equivalent outcomes across diverse psychotherapies, and this effect has been dubbed the "Dodo effect" (Rosenzweig, 1936). When all psychotherapy methods are found to have equally beneficial effects, 'everyone wins the race, and all get a prize,' akin to the verdict of the Dodo bird in *Alice in Wonderland* (Carroll, 1971/1865). This effect has been explained in several ways, including (a) the notion that therapeutic change owes more to common factors than to specific factors in a particular psychotherapy approach, (b) the notion that different psychotherapies may lead to comparable outcomes through different pathways, and (c) methodological problems (Grawe, 1997; Lambert, 2013b).

Within this context, *specificity* refers to the extent to which particular treatment components, mechanisms, or techniques are directly linked to specific therapeutic outcomes. Specificity in psychotherapy research is crucial to identifying which techniques drive specific outcomes, but its complexity lies in isolating these effects from common factors and individual client differences. An early effort to conceptualize therapeutic change factors in psychodrama identified the following six: emotional abreaction/release, cognitive insight, behavioral learning, interpersonal relationships, nonspecific healing aids, and the therapist's qualities (Kellermann, 1987b, pp. 410–411). Emotional abreaction and cognitive insight were perceived as the most helpful factors by psychodrama group members, whereas the control group identified nonspecific healing aids as the most helpful. However, these categories are more generic than uniquely specific to psychodrama, as they are applicable to numerous other therapeutic approaches and do not highlight distinct drama-based therapeutic factors. Specificity is essential when formulating a *theory of change*, which posits an explanation of how and why a particular therapeutic intervention leads to desired changes in a person's thoughts, emotions, behaviors, and/or overall well-being. A theory of change in psychodrama would outline how psychodrama brings about a desired outcome and detail the processes through which change occurs. A *specific change factor* is thus a well-specified therapeutic change factor that is theorized to produce therapeutic benefits in a specific psychotherapy approach, such as psychodrama (de Witte et al., 2021).

Some researchers have reported that common and specific factors exhibit significant correlations, thus indicating that they are not entirely independent (de Felice et al., 2019). For example, a protagonist's action insight (a specific psychodrama change factor described below) may emerge due to the *strong alliance* between the therapist and the protagonist or because the protagonist has high *expectations and motivation* for change (two common factors). Therefore, it is essential to examine how common and specific factors interact within a comprehensive theory of change, which should coherently outline the sequence and direction of their effects. Finally, while a change factor is a single component that accounts for a therapeutic effect, it may not explain the mechanism of change in detail. Rather, a change factor can indicate a potential mechanism without directly being one itself (Kazdin, 2009).

6.2 Mechanisms of Change

Change factors (common and specific) differ from *mechanisms of change*. Whereas the former refers to a single component that accounts for a therapeutic effect, the latter is a more complex concept. In pharmacological research, "mechanism of action" refers to the specific causal and biochemical ways in which a drug produces effects in the body. In psychotherapy research, the term "mechanism of change" is more commonly used to refer to "the processes or events that are responsible for the change; the reasons why change occurred or how change came about" (Kazdin, 2009, p. 419). In other words, a mechanism of change is a causal sequence comprising two or more interacting factors that lead to and are responsible for the outcome or change (de Witte et al., 2021).

Carey et al. (2020) conducted a scoping review and concluded that "mechanisms in the psychotherapy field are discussed almost exclusively in conceptual or statistical terms" (p. 7) that often lack precision and sufficient clarity. They called for researchers to examine *functional mechanisms* involving neurobiological brain processes expressed in precise (mathematical) functional terms. They argued that without a functional mechanism, it is difficult to determine the extent to which they are distinct or overlapping and differentiate between a mechanism and its outcomes or effects. For instance, should increased emotion regulation and decreased anxiety be identified as mechanisms of change or as the consequences of neurobiological or physiological[16] mechanistic processes? Moreover, because psychotherapy is a *complex intervention* that involves many interacting components (Skivington et al., 2021), change process research should explore how therapists and protagonists co-create positive outcomes. Along these lines, psychodrama researchers must develop criteria for functional mechanisms of change to lead to a robust mechanistic account of the change process. In the final section of this Element, I explore the psychophysiological and neurobiological processes frequently utilized in psychotherapy research, to inspire new directions for future mechanistic research in psychodrama and drama therapy.

---

[16] *Neurobiological* refers specifically to the biological mechanisms of the brain and nervous system, while *physiological* encompasses a broader range of biological processes occurring throughout the entire body. See section 7.

6.3 Change Factors in Psychodrama

This section discusses eleven practice-based change factors derived from documented psychodrama practices, which are theorized to facilitate therapeutic change in psychodrama. They do not constitute an exhaustive list.

Dramatic engagement refers to the extent to which protagonists who have transitioned from the ordinary reality to the surplus (psychodramatic) reality sustain their active participation and immersion in the dramatic activities in a session. These activities include role-playing, verbal, aural, and physical expressions, creative and projective work guided by the psychodramatist, and interactions with other group members when applicable (Frydman et al., 2022; Orkibi et al., 2017). Dramatic engagement is a construct that corresponds to evidence on the significant role of client involvement in psychotherapy change process research (Morris et al., 2016).

Relatedly, *embodiment* concerns how protagonists express their emotions, thoughts, and sensations through physical postures, gestures, and movements, thereby externalizing inner experiences physically, both consciously and unconsciously. Embodiment allows protagonists to tune into their bodily experiences and unspoken feelings, thus highlighting the potential differences between a covert "embodied self" and an overt "narrative self" (Scorolli, 2019). Embodiment promotes kinaesthetic body awareness and emphasizes the body-mind connection (Frydman et al., 2022). Its nonverbal nature helps release tension and energy (de Witte et al., 2021) and uncover the invisible traces embedded in the mind and body by the biochemical, physiological, and anatomic effects of past adverse experiences (van der Kolk, 2014). Embodiment in psychodrama can access what Gendlin (1996) described as the "felt sense," a preverbal, subtle, and vague yet direct bodily awareness (i.e., holistic embodied knowing) of one's inner state concerning an issue, situation, or experience. By bringing focused attention to the felt sense and approaching it with friendly curiosity, the protagonist can identify "a word, phrase, image, gesture, or sound that matches, symbolizes, or describes the felt sense" (Rappaport, 2008, p. 31) that can then be externalized and concretized, as described below.

In its basic form, embodiment is reality-based, such as when protagonists enact (embody) someone from their lives (e.g., role-playing their father) or express inner voices. However, the arts, including drama, ascribe symbolic form to a broad range of human feelings (Langer, 1953). Therefore, in other cases, embodiment can be *metaphoric* and *symbolic expressions* that deliver succinct implicit messages about the protagonists' inner experiences and sensations and convey the maximum meaning of rich inner experiences with a minimum of words (Ronen, 2011). For instance, "I am standing at the edge of a cliff" is often used metaphorically to depict a feeling of precariousness or danger. It conveys a sense of vulnerability and uncertainty, as though the person were on the verge of something transformative or life-altering. Similarly, a protagonist who says, "I carry the world on my shoulders" metaphorically expresses feeling burdened by heavy responsibilities, problems, or worries. This statement typically conveys the experience of shouldering an overwhelming load, and often implies a sense of feeling weighed down by life's challenges or obligations. Metaphoric and symbolic expressions, which are often enacted through psychodramatic imagery, bypass rational thought and typically help bring subconscious material into conscious awareness (Imus, 2021) and facilitate meaning-making (Jones, 2021).

Externalization-concretization refers to the process of externalizing intangible inner psychological states, which are often difficult to articulate or comprehend, into a tangible and visible dramatic form that can thus be physically perceived, experienced, and related to (Kushnir & Orkibi, 2021). Read-Johnson (1998) argued that during therapeutic action, "inner states are externalized or projected into the arts media, transformed in health-promoting ways, and then re-internalized by the client" (p. 85). In psychodrama, intangible inner content is externalized and made concrete using external objects, such as role players, an empty chair, or projective therapeutic cards. In this context, *embodied concretization* is where protagonists physically enact and express their (externalized) inner experiences and emotions through self-presentation.

The externalization of inner psychological states facilitates *perspective-taking* (Malhotra et al., 2024), the attempt to understand another person's thoughts, feelings, motivations, and experiences (Davis, 1983). In psychodrama, the main technique that induces perspective-taking is role-reversal, followed by doubling and mirroring (Kipper & Ben-Ely, 1979; Soysal, 2023). By seeing things from another person's viewpoint, protagonists develop greater empathy and understanding for others, which often leads to better communication and healthier relationships. Understanding the perspectives of others enhances individuals' self-awareness of their own behaviors and their impact on others, thereby supporting better emotion regulation.

Spontaneity is a state of readiness that propels "the individual towards an adequate response to a new situation or a new response to an old situation" (Moreno, 1953, p. 42). Warming up protagonists' spontaneity is crucial for fueling adaptive responses to life situations. Spontaneity is experienced at varying degrees of intensity, which are manifested in several physiological indices: the "heart rate may be increased, the pulse may be more rapid, respiration rate increased, etc." (Moreno, 1955b, p. 112). These physiological processes may be further explored to disentangle the mechanisms of change underlying spontaneity.

Psychodrama, and its warm-up phase in particular, often facilitates a playful experience, which is frequently induced by activities such as improvisation or theater games that frame or reframe (cf. Barnett, 2007) the therapeutic situation as fun, amusing, or entertaining and, therefore, nonthreatening. The experience of *playfulness*[17] is intrinsically motivating and is characterized by openness to self-exploration, expression, and receptivity. Playfulness thus encourages not only self-understanding but also interpersonal connections (Shen & Masek, 2024). Blatner (1996) argued that embracing playfulness helps avoid becoming overly attached to the outcome of each action. It is worth noting that playfulness does not denote frivolity or superficial humor, since protagonists may also engage in "play" with difficult emotional experiences within the psychodramatic (surplus) reality that serves as the therapeutic container (J. L. Moreno, 1965; Pendzik, 2006). As protagonists are transported into this playful space, they experience a temporary liberation from external constraints that allows them to explore new possibilities and new ways of being in the world (Feniger-Schaal et al., 2024). This process in psychodrama shares similarities with the distancing-embracing model on the emotional effects of aesthetic experiences that emphasizes the role of psychological distancing in creating a perceived separation between an individual and specific emotion, experience, or stimulus (Menninghaus et al., 2017). This separation enables the individual to experience negative emotions more safely and constructively. In psychodrama, psychological distancing is achieved by cognitively framing experiences as part of a representational role-play in a "fail-safe" surplus reality. This framing provides personal safety and control over the continuation or cessation of the emotional experience, thus facilitating the exploration and processing of a wide range of emotional responses in the psychodramatic here-and-now.

Central to psychodrama is the concept of role, which is the tangible manifestation of one's self in a specific situation. In this context, another therapeutic change factor is *role distancing*, which facilitates a separation between protagonists and a maladaptive role they play in life (Blatner, 1991). Instigating protagonists' ability to disidentify (i.e., differentiate themselves) from their maladaptive behaviors by stepping back and reflecting on their actions is conceptualized in psychodrama as taking on what Blatner (2006) termed the "meta-role," the choosing self. This helps the protagonist connect with a broader meta-role that can reflect on, reassess, redefine, and renegotiate one's role repertoire for better adaptation and optimal functioning (Azoulay & Orkibi, 2015).

---

[17] The conceptualization presented here differs from the idea of playfulness as an individual trait that predisposes a person to participate in play behaviors (see Shen & Masek, 2023).

Relatedly, *role reconstruction and expansion* refer to the extent to which protagonists can explore various roles as tangible representations of themselves (Bucuță et al., 2018), consistent with the idea that expanding one's role repertoire enables flexible movement between roles and, therefore, adaptation to the needs of a given situation (Azoulay & Orkibi, 2015; Blatner, 1991; Keisari, 2021).

People frequently turn to psychodrama to resolve intra- and interpersonal issues. Psychodramatically, this is conceptualized as an act-hunger for act fulfillment that stems from humans' innate drive for healing by embodying the completeness of an action (Blatner, 2000b). Therefore, psychodrama often involves *active catharsis*, which consists of three elements, according to Kellermann (1984). The first element is the discharge of intense feelings blocked or repressed through active participation in dramatic enactment within a supportive therapeutic environment. This change factor builds on the premise that unexpressed emotions accumulate, similar to steam in a pressure cooker, leading to internal pressure or tension, which in turn contributes to psychological dysfunction. To restore well-being, protagonists must release this emotional buildup through expression, which is commonly known as catharsis (Kellermann, 1984). The second element suggests that active catharsis involves emotional release that is "preceded, accompanied, or followed by ... a *cognitive release* of an idea from the unconscious" (Kellermann, 1984, p. 4. emphasis added). Therefore, active catharsis includes experiencing *action insight*, where a deeper understanding of underlying issues is achieved through active exploration. The third element of action catharsis entails *actional release*, in which the emotional residues of intrapsychic tensions are translated into observable behavior. In other words, ideally, an active catharsis is not solely emotional and cognitive; rather, it is embodied and experienced through the immersive enactment of psychodrama (Kellermann, 1984).

Overall, this section explored eleven practice-based change factors that point to the ways in which psychodrama leads to change. The next sections discuss qualitative and quantitative research methods that can be applied to change process research in psychodrama.

6.4 Qualitative Methods for Change Process Research

A recent review of research in the last ten years indicates that qualitative methods, which provide a rich understanding of human experience, are generally less frequent in psychotherapy change process research than quantitative ones (Krause, 2024). Qualitative change process research in psychotherapy often focuses on *significant events*; namely, pivotal moments or interactions within therapy sessions that clients or therapists identify as especially meaningful, impactful, or therapeutic. These events may include both helpful and hindering experiences.

Early process researchers relied solely on therapists' notes to document what occurred during therapy sessions. Today, however, a widely used qualitative method for studying psychotherapy change processes involves the *Helpful Aspects of Therapy* (HAT) form (Elliott, 2010; Llewelyn, 1988). This form is a primarily qualitative post-session questionnaire that allows clients to report their experiences of helpful and hindering events, thus providing immediate documentation of in-session significant events. The *Brief Structured Recall* is a video-assisted procedure where clients use the HAT form to identify significant events from their sessions, then review the corresponding moments in the video recording and reflect on them with the researcher (Elliott & Shapiro, 1988). This approach minimizes recall bias and enhances the richness of the data. In psychodrama, it can be applied to explore associations between specific techniques or processes and both session-level and treatment-level outcomes. Another instrument, the *Client Change Interview*, is an open-ended interview administered after treatment termination to collect detailed data on clients' overall experiences and perceptions of change throughout therapy, including helpful and hindering events. For the full version, see Elliott and Rodgers (2008), and for the abridged version, see Elliott (2012).

Timulak (2010) identified two approaches to analyzing significant events in psychotherapy research. Researchers can use *thematic analysis* (Braun & Clarke, 2021)[18] to identify and develop recurring patterns of meaning (themes) in their data to reveal different types of significant events. Alternatively, they can leverage existing *event taxonomies* from previous research, by adopting them entirely or adapting them to their specific treatment and study (e.g., Castonguay et al., 2010; Elliott et al., 1985; Llewelyn et al., 1988; Martin & Stelmaczonek, 1988). One such taxonomy is Cruz and colleagues' (2016) Helpful Aspects of Morenian Psychodrama Content Analysis System (HAMPCAS) based on data collected from the HAT form. The system consists of three domains: a 17-item Action/Technique domain that covers what the protagonist, psychodramatist, or group members did during the event that gave rise to its impact; a 23-item Impact domain that charts the effects of the event on the protagonist, with categories divided into helpful (e.g., alliance strengthening) and hindering (e.g., unwanted experiences) impact; and a 8-item Content domain that relates to what/who the event was about (e.g., family of origin).

---

[18] See also www.thematicanalysis.net/.

Unlike thematic analysis, which organizes data into patterned themes or event taxonomies, which uses pre-existing events, *grounded theory* (see Bryant & Charmaz, 2007; O'Callaghan, 2012) is particularly well-suited for building a data-driven theory of change in psychodrama because it focuses on constructing an explanatory framework that uncovers underlying processes and dynamic interactions between factors (e.g., common and specific), rather than merely describing themes.

Overall, by employing these qualitative methods, psychodrama researchers can gain a deeper understanding of the protagonist's and therapist's perspectives on the significant events and processes that lead to or hinder therapeutic change, including the immediate process outcome of the techniques used.

6.5 Quantitative Methods for Change Process Research

In RCT designs, symptom evaluations are typically conducted pre- and post-treatment, where changes are analyzed based on group averages. Because this approach fails to capture the dynamic, nonlinear nature of change during treatment, more frequent assessments are needed to examine change trajectories throughout therapy (Hayes et al., 2008). In addition, the temporal precedence of changes in process variables over changes in outcome variables should be established (Kazdin, 2009).

One of the major hurdles in psychodrama change process research is the lack of quantitative research tools. Recently steps have been taken to develop reliable self-report and observational tools that can assess the presence of specific drama-based therapeutic factors during sessions that can account for changes in outcomes. One example is the *Dramatic Engagement Scale*, which measures the extent to which a protagonist is engaged in a dramatic activity during a session, according to the therapist's evaluation (Orkibi et al., 2017). Another example is our new self-report *State Spontaneity Scale*, which is designed to measure spontaneity consistent with Morenos' conceptualization of this construct as a pre-creative state (Biancalani & Orkibi, 2025). We have also developed four self-report tools that have shown promising preliminary results (Elkarif et al., 2024): the *Drama Intervention Alliance Inventory* (adapted from Bat Or & Zilcha-Mano, 2019), the *Satet Flow in Drama Intervention Scale* (adapted from Martin & Jackson, 2008), the *Meaningfulness in Drama Intervention Scale* (adapted from Baker et al., 2016), and the *Perceived Group Social Support Scale* (adapted from Koenig et al., 1993). These questionnaires can provide valuable insights into protagonists' experiences during psychodrama sessions through quantitative analysis. In addition to self-reports,

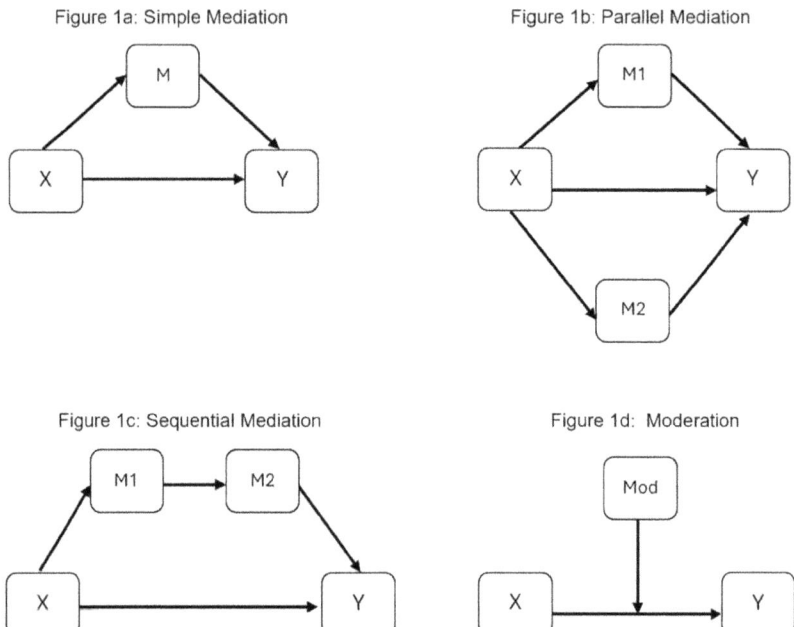

Figure 1 Types of Mediation and Moderation Models

Note. X = independent variable (mostly the form of therapy or intervention), M = Mediator (the change factor operationalized into a mediator), Y = dependent variable/outcome (e.g., stress), Mod = Moderator. For additional mediation and moderation models, see Hayes (2013).

video-recorded sessions offer rich observable data that researchers can analyze using quantitative coding schemes and rating scales currently in the initial stages of development.

Quantitative research in psychotherapy is increasingly exploring mediation and moderation to move beyond basic questions of effectiveness (Kazdin, 2009, 2014). A *mediator* is a variable that accounts for the indirect association between an intervention and an outcome. In other words, a mediator (M) is an intervening variable theorized to account for the causal statistical relationship between two variables, such that X causes M, which in turn causes Y (see Figure 1a). In psychotherapy research, a mediator is often situated between the intervention (independent variable, X) and the outcome (dependent variable, Y) (Kazdin, 2009). For example, a psychodrama intervention (X) may decrease self-criticism (Y) through an increase in self-compassion (M).

A more complex change theory can have parallel mediators or a chain of sequential mediators in a single statistical model, as illustrated in Figures 1b and 1c, respectively. It is possible to examine a change theory where the predictor variable (*X*) is the common change factor, followed by a sequence of other change factors leading to the outcome. One example is Shechtman and Leichtentritt's (2010) study on the association of processes with outcomes in child group therapy, as well as the illustrative example below.

Note that mediation is not equivalent to a mechanism because isolating a mediator does not itself explain how treatment leads to change. Kazdin (2009) noted that while the study of mediation is the first step toward understanding how therapy works, "a mechanism refers to a greater level of specificity than a mediator and reflects the steps or processes through which therapy (or some independent variable) actually unfolds and produces the change" (p. 419). Proposing a mechanism of change is, first and foremost, a theoretical endeavor that should reflect the theory of change posited by the researcher. This includes a causal sequence of mediators (in quantitative mediation analysis) that reflect how the change occurred. To date, there are no evidence-based explanations of precisely why psychodrama works and how it leads to changes. Future studies should pinpoint mediators that might account for treatment effects based on theoretical reasoning.

A *moderator* is a construct external to the treatment that influences the direction or magnitude of the relationship between the intervention and outcome, which can lead to a better understanding of "when" or "for whom" therapy leads to change, as can be seen in *Figure 1d* (Frazier et al., 2004). Moderators are often client or therapist characteristics (e.g., gender, ethnicity, trait, temperament), treatment delivery format (e.g., individual vs. group treatment, in-person vs. online), or frequency (e.g., once vs. twice a week) (Kazdin, 2009, 2014). More sophisticated statistical methods can explore a moderated mediation model where the relationship between X and Y through M is moderated by (or "conditioned on") one or more variables, where the mediation effect varies depending on specific individuals or contexts (Hayes, 2013, pp. xi, 432).

In terms of quantitative data analysis, in addition to mediation and moderation analyses (Hayes, 2013; Preacher et al., 2010), *growth curve modeling*[19] (Hayes et al., 2008) and *multilevel modeling*[20] (Peugh, 2010) can enhance psychodrama process research by allowing researchers to explore longitudinal

---

[19] Growth curve modeling is a statistical technique used to analyze change over time. It is often applied in longitudinal studies where data are collected at multiple time points from the same individuals or groups. It allows researchers to examine and model individual trajectories of change, such as growth, decline, or stability, in variables of interest over time.

[20] Multilevel modeling (MLM), also known as hierarchical linear modeling or mixed-effects modeling, is a statistical technique for analyzing data with a hierarchical or nested structure. It is particularly useful when data points are not independent but grouped into clusters (e.g., patients within hospitals).

changes within individuals and variations across different groups or settings. Overcoming the challenge of limited quantitative measures is crucial, and developing reliable measures of drama-based therapeutic factors during sessions would constitute a significant step forward. This would lead to deeper insights through quantitative analysis and enable the exploration of mediation and moderation effects, thus advancing the study of psychodrama's mechanisms of change and its impact on outcomes.

Illustrative Example

This example presents a potential theory of change in self-compassion psychodrama. It is grounded in evidence that self-compassion enhances well-being by modulating psychophysiological responses to stress (Slivjak et al., 2023), which include increased heart rate variability, reduced cortisol levels, and changes in brain activity linked to emotion regulation and the stress response (Anthes & Dreisoerner, 2024). The theoretical model proposes three sequential mediators for quantitative process research. The predictor, the *therapeutic alliance* (*Predictor variable*), is a common factor in psychotherapy that reflects the relationship between the psychodramatist and the protagonist (Elkarif et al., 2024). A strong alliance is theorized to catalyze protagonists' *spontaneity* (*Mediator 1*), a specific factor in psychodrama that enhances their ability to respond flexibly and creatively (Biancalani & Orkibi, 2025). Increased spontaneity, in turn, is theorized to trigger active *dramatic engagement* (*Mediator 2*), another specific factor in psychodrama (Orkibi et al., 2017). In self-compassion psychodrama, this engagement focuses on exploring and enacting the dynamics between the self-critic and the criticized self, which is often accompanied by significant physiological arousal. However, within the holding and containing surplus reality, introducing the compassionate self helps the protagonists regulate, tolerate, and process the emotions arising from these enacted dynamics. This progression toward greater self-compassion and reduced self-criticism is further theorized to activate the *parasympathetic nervous system* (*Mediator 3*), which is associated with reduced *cortisol levels* (Cowand et al., 2024; Herriot et al., 2018) and increased *activity in the frontopolar cortex*, a region believed to be actively involved in self-compassionate thinking, and which can be measured with fNIRS[21] (dos Santos et al., 2022). Ultimately, this process is theorized to increase self-compassion (a session-level *outcome variable*), which has been associated with a range of mental health outcomes (Neff, 2023). This illustration thus integrates psychological and physiological mediators to

---

[21] fNIRS is a non-invasive neuroimaging technique used to measure changes in brain activity by monitoring blood oxygenation levels in the brain.

constitute a detailed account of the speculated change processes in self-compassion psychodrama.

7 The Road Ahead

This final section discusses uncharted territories in psychodrama research to inspire new directions for future research in the field. Technological and methodological developments have advanced research on the roles of interpersonal synchrony, psychophysiological, and neurobiological processes in psychotherapy. These lines of psychotherapy research can uncover phenomena that are challenging to capture using traditional self-report or observational methods, and can result in a more precise analysis of an individual's response to treatment, thereby shedding new light on the mechanisms underlying therapeutic change (Atzil-Slonim, 2024).

7.1 Nonverbal Body Movement Synchrony

Given the crucial role played by the therapeutic relationship in successful therapy, researchers have increasingly examined its relation to synchrony between patient and therapist, consistent with the view that synchrony is an evolutionary-based mechanism that facilitates social cohesion and bonding (Zilcha-Mano, 2024, p. 2). Accordingly, the prevailing theoretical assumption in psychotherapy research is that robust synchrony between therapists and clients correlates with a stronger therapeutic alliance and more favorable treatment outcomes (Zilcha-Mano, 2024). This synchrony is considered a potential mechanism driving therapeutic change and is characterized by elements of co-regulation and shared experience (Prinz et al., 2022) that involve physiological synchrony, as discussed below. However, synchrony is not limited to attunement, co-regulation, and downregulation; it can also manifest as mutual escalation or amplification and should be considered alongside desynchrony. This underscores "the value of therapists being attentive to nonverbal cues and moving flexibly in and out of synchrony" (Atzil-Slonim et al., 2023, p. 898).

Nonverbal coordinated body movements are the most basic form of interpersonal synchrony in psychotherapy (Koole & Tschacher, 2016), followed by synchrony of voice, emotions, and physiological and neurobiological processes. *Nonverbal synchrony* refers to the coordination of movements between interacting individuals regardless of the specific postures or gestures they display (Cohen et al., 2021). Researchers focus on how these movements change over time and how they align or synchronize with each other during interactions. This nonverbal synchrony can be studied by a range of methods, including moment-to-moment observational coding of video recordings or motion capture technology (Ramseyer, 2020). For example, research has shown that nonverbal synchrony is associated with a strong therapist-client relationship and a stronger sense of self-efficacy in clients (Ramseyer & Tschacher, 2011). In a different study, more synchrony predicted lower interpersonal problem scores at the end of therapy (Altmann et al., 2020). However, the results for nonverbal synchrony are inconsistent (see reviews in Atzil-Slonim et al., 2023; Wessler et al., 2024), possibly due to the fact that studies have failed to differentiate between stable trait-like nonverbal synchrony and changes in state-like nonverbal synchrony that occur during treatment (Cohen et al., 2021).

In a novel theoretical model for psychotherapy synchronization research, Zlicha-Mano (2024) posited that synchrony has both trait-like and state-like components that are complementary. Going in as well as going out of sync have potential therapeutic benefits in correcting maladaptive trait-like tendencies related to synchronization. In other words, when a state-like synchronization intervention induces a deviation from the client's (maladaptive) stable trait-like tendency to get in sync, these changes can be therapeutic because they may gradually cultivate a more adaptive state-like tendency. This theoretical model focuses on dyadic interaction, which in psychodrama can involve the protagonist-psychodramatist and/or protagonist-auxiliary ego dyads. Zlicha-Mano's model also holds potential for group settings despite the increased complexity. While studies in other fields have connected group synchrony and coherence (e.g., Tomashin et al., 2022), there is scant research on synchrony in group psychotherapy.

7.2 Vocal Arousal and Synchrony

Vocal communication of emotion refers to "the process wherein speakers express emotions by modulating nonverbal aspects of their speech, and listeners utilize the nonverbal aspects of speech to make inferences about the emotional experience of the speaker" (Laukka, 2017, p. 1). *Vocal arousal* refers to fluctuations in pitch (highness or lowness of a sound), amplitude (loudness), pace, and other acoustic features of the voice that reflect emotional states such as excitement, stress, or agitation. Research linking voice and emotions has mainly focused on vocal pitch and amplitude to examine listeners' inferences about a vocalizer's emotional state from speech acoustics (Bachorowski & Owren, 2008). *Vocal synchrony*, on the other hand, refers to the coordination of vocal patterns between the therapist and the client during interactions.

The analyses of vocal arousal and vocal synchrony play vital roles in understanding the dynamics of therapeutic interactions. Voice analysis in psychotherapy research is used to assess both intrapersonal and interpersonal affect dynamics, which take place simultaneously in both the client and therapist (Paz et al., 2021, p. 229). For example, one study found a significant positive correlation between vocal pitch synchrony and observed therapist empathy (Imel et al., 2014). In a study by Reich et al. (2014), greater therapist-leading synchrony was associated with significantly lower ratings of the therapeutic alliance, suggesting that when therapists lead pitch shifts, clients may feel less connected or understood. In contrast, greater therapist-following synchrony was related to higher reports of client depression, indicating that when therapists match the client's pitch, it may reflect or amplify the client's distress. Atzil-Slonim et al. (2023) observed that the client's and therapist's vocal arousal may rise and fall together in synchrony and that the therapist can use co-regulation to help the client move toward a more stable arousal level. Overall, vocal pitch synchrony in psychotherapy is a subtle phenomenon that may not be as impactful as other forms of nonverbal synchrony such as body movement (Reich et al., 2014). Nevertheless, studying vocal synchrony in psychodrama can provide valuable insights into the dynamics of verbal-emotional expression and therapeutic communication among the protagonist, the auxiliary ego, and the psychodramatist.

7.3 Face Reading

Face reading (FR) analyzes facial expressions and cues to understand emotional states, psychological processes, and interpersonal dynamics during therapeutic interactions. FR software is a noninvasive wireless method that uses facial recognition technology to automatically analyze facial expressions moment-by-moment, unlike self-reports that offer a limited retrospective view and cannot fully capture emotional dynamics during a session. FR software has proved to be a valuable method to objectively evaluate whether psychotherapy can help clients engage in emotion regulation to alleviate the experience of negative emotions (Arango et al., 2019). There is initial evidence that artificial intelligence-based facial expression analysis can detect in-session emotional dynamics that predict decreased depressive symptoms (Fisher et al., 2023). Incorporating FR technology into psychodrama research could provide valuable insights into how the protagonist's emotional dynamics change in response to specific procedures or techniques. FR data can also be linked to other process measures, such as spontaneity (Biancalani & Orkibi, 2025) or the therapeutic alliance (Horvath & Greenberg, 1989), and explored for associations with outcomes at both the session and treatment levels.

7.4 Physiological Avenues

The field of psychology has been utilizing psychophysiological measurements for several decades (for a review see Tassinary et al., 2012). *Psychophysiology* generally refers to the physiological manifestations of psychological processes and behavior and the influence of psychological interventions on physiological responses. Psychophysiology can uncover bodily phenomena that are difficult to capture using traditional self-report or observational methods, thus resulting in a more precise analysis of an individual's physiological response to treatment, which can shed light on the underlying mechanisms of change (Atzil-Slonim, 2024). The most commonly used physiological measures in psychotherapy research include:

- *Heart rate (HR) and heart rate variability (HRV)*: These measures assess fluctuations in the time intervals between heartbeats as measured by electrocardiography (ECG or EKG). This is done by placing electrodes on the chest to detect the electrical activity of the heart. HR and HRV reflect the activity of the autonomic nervous system (ANS) and offer insights into stress levels and emotional regulation. The ANS comprises the sympathetic nervous system, which activates the body's fight-or-flight response, and the parasympathetic nervous system, which promotes relaxation and recovery ("rest and digest"). An increase in HR typically indicates sympathetic activation associated with heightened vigilance, active avoidance behavior, and negative affect ("fight or flight"). Conversely, HR decreases with parasympathetic activation, suggesting a positive effect. The vagus nerve, a vital component of the parasympathetic nervous system, plays a major role in regulating HR. HRV explicitly reflects the balance between sympathetic and parasympathetic influences on the heart, where higher HRV indicates greater adaptability and resilience to stress. There is evidence that anxiety and depression are associated with low HRV (Kirby et al., 2017) and that compassion-focused therapy, which includes imagery-based guided exercises, can directly increase HRV as a marker of the parasympathetic nervous system's response (Di Bello et al., 2020; Kim et al., 2024). A significant positive correlation was found between HRV and client-perceived therapeutic presence, which involves "the feeling of being received, understood, and safe in therapy" and was shown to be associated with the client's parasympathetic nervous system (Deits-Lebehn et al., 2020, p. 490). Incorporating HR and HRV measurements in psychodrama research can help show how psychodramatic techniques (e.g., containing double; Hudgins & Drucker, 1998; Hudgins & Toscani, 2014) influence emotion regulation and contribute to its overall effectiveness in reducing arousal.

- *Respiration rate and respiratory sinus arrhythmia (RSA)*: These measures serve to assess breathing patterns and respiratory variability linked to emotional regulation and stress reduction. Evidence shows that controlled slow breathing correlates with increased HRV (Steffen et al., 2021; Zaccaro et al., 2018). One example is the use of soothing rhythmic breathing in the "cultivating the compassionate self" exercise in compassion-focused therapy (Kim et al., 2024, p. 2). In terms of interpersonal physiological synchrony, therapist-client synchrony in breathing patterns and the subsequent co-regulation (i.e., modulation) of HR and HRV has been theorized to be associated with therapeutic alliance quality that, in turn, may foster the client's capacity for emotion regulation (Koole & Tschacher, 2016).
- *Skin conductance*: This measure, also known as electrodermal activity (EDA) and galvanic skin response (GSR), assesses changes in the electrical activity of the skin (i.e., increased sweat) as an indicator of emotional arousal and stress levels associated with the sympathetic nervous system. It is measured via electrodes attached to the hands. Psychotherapy studies show that skin conductance can provide insights into the quality of the therapist-client therapeutic alliance. For example, higher synchrony between the therapist's and client's EDA correlated with the client-rated therapist's empathy and positive social-emotional processes (Marci et al., 2007). In an imagery-based treatment, interpersonal synchrony in EDA was significantly associated with the bonding aspect of the therapeutic alliance (Bar-Kalifa et al., 2019). Other studies have shown that EDA synchrony during image-rescripting interventions predicted lower post-treatment test anxiety (Prinz et al., 2022), and that skin conductance synchrony can predict image therapy effectiveness, as indicated by a change in the severity of symptoms in a follow-up assessment (Gernert et al., 2024). Psychodrama researchers can use EDA to measure the intensity and duration of emotional responses to different psychodrama techniques.
- *Cortisol levels*: Cortisol is the "stress hormone," in that elevated cortisol levels in saliva or hair samples can indicate heightened stress, anxiety, or other factors triggering the body's stress response. Cortisol levels fluctuate throughout the day, peak after waking, and decrease later on. Women may experience increased cortisol reactivity during ovulation. Factors such as exercise, eating, smoking, and social stress also impact cortisol levels (Fischer & Zilcha-Mano, 2022). In psychotherapy research, cortisol is the most well-researched of all hormones. Some studies have shown that psychotherapy can reduce cortisol levels for clients with depression as well as for those with generalized anxiety disorder (Fischer & Zilcha-Mano, 2022). In a recent study, the interdependence of cortisol (i.e., the arousal biomarker)

between therapists and clients was dependent on the quality of the client-rated therapist-client alliance, such that in a poorer alliance, there was a stronger association between the client's pre-session and their therapist's post-session cortisol levels (Levi et al., 2024). This dynamic underscores the role of a good alliance in protecting the client's emotional states from becoming contagious, which can negatively impact both the client and the therapist. A recent experiment with older adults suggested that during improvisational playful interaction, uncertainty levels rise (Golland et al., 2024; Golland et al., 2025), which prompts the activation of the noradrenergic cortical arousal system (related to alertness, attention, and cognitive arousal), which can be seen through changes in skin conductance responses. This activation was associated with improved cognitive performance.

- *Oxytocin levels*: Oxytocin is a neurotransmitter in the brain stimulated by interpersonal cues in safe situations and is sometimes more loosely referred to as the "love/bonding hormone" due to its role in approach and reciprocity, emotion recognition, social bonding, trust, empathy, compassion, and mother-infant attachment (Zilcha-Mano et al., 2020). In psychotherapy research, oxytocin is often measured in saliva samples. Emerging evidence suggests that synchrony between patients' and therapists' oxytocin levels is associated with effective treatment (Zilcha-Mano et al., 2020). In a different study, clients who presented higher oxytocin reactivity during a therapeutic session experienced greater improvement in depressive symptoms throughout treatment (Atzil-Slonim et al., 2022). Initial evidence from a recent experiment with older adults indicated that a fifteen-minute playful interaction with the mirror game (an improvisational exercise based on dyadic synchronized movement) that was experienced as positive led to an increase in levels of saliva oxytocin, which was associated with a reduction in loneliness (Abu Elheja et al., 2021).

7.5 Neurobiological Avenues

All forms of psychotherapy aim to enhance the integration of neural networks (Cozolino, 2014), and since the brain is an action-oriented organ, "it should not be surprising that its integrative potential is realized through action" (Hug, 2007, p. 227).

7.5.1 Psychodrama and Neuroscience

While there is little research on the neuroscience of psychodrama, several theoretical perspectives have emerged. According to Hug (2007), during the action phase of psychodrama, the protagonist mildly regresses to an earlier developmental stage, which is associated with a reduction in the inhibitory function of the prefrontal cortex, the brain area responsible for higher-order cognitive functions such as decision-making, problem-solving, planning, impulse control, and regulating social behavior. The action phase also involves "the activation of right brain emotional structures through scene setting, imagery and motion within the space of the stage, and connecting this activation with left brain structures through verbalization" (p. 234). Hug's conceptualization encompasses the "cerebral lateralization" (right–left) paradigm and the "front–back" (frontal lobe–corticolimbic system) paradigm. Accordingly, healing involves both the integration of the left and right hemispheres (responsible for logic and speech, and emotion and images, respectively) and the connections between the prefrontal cortex and the corticolimbic system (responsible for regulation and decision-making, and emotion and memory, respectively).

Hug (2013) further suggested that trauma-informed psychodrama can facilitate neural integration by reconnecting the prefrontal cortex and the limbic system, which may become dysregulated after trauma. They also argued that trauma involves right-brain hyperactivation and left-brain hypoactivation, resulting in bodily paralysis. To address this issue, psychodrama seeks to facilitate experiential integration by guiding individuals to consciously revisit past traumas within their subjective *window of tolerance* –that is, individuals' optimal state of arousal where they can effectively cope with stress and regulate their emotions (Siegel, 1999). This process entails bringing traumatic experiences into the present moment by allowing for emotional expression that engages the right brain's emotional processing while simultaneously promoting self-soothing, containment, and a sense of safety to calm the amygdala and reduce cortisol levels to prevent the flooding of overwhelming emotions. This brain-balanced approach enables the rational and language-oriented left brain to engage in sense-making, thus facilitating the integration of traumatic experiences into a coherent narrative memory in the service of the ego. These neurobiological considerations are echoed in what Dayton (2016) termed *neuropsychodrama*, "a trauma-informed approach to psychodrama that pays particular attention to relational moments of reliving that emerge during a role play" (p. 41).

Bilik (2019) similarly posited that psychodrama activates various brain regions[22] and that when individuals engage in psychodrama and recall bodily

---

[22] These include the prefrontal cortex (executive function), amygdala (emotion processing, fear response), hippocampus (memory formation, spatial navigation), dorsal raphe nucleus (serotonin production, mood regulation), and locus coeruleus (norepinephrine production, stress response) (Bilik, 2019).

memories, they may access deep-seated, primal experiences stored in subcortical brain structures, such as the *limbic system*, which is responsible for forming and storing memories, processing emotions, motivating behavior, managing stress responses, and facilitating social connections.[23] As these memories are processed and brought to conscious awareness, neuronal activity extends from these subcortical regions to the *prefrontal cortex*. This process facilitates enhanced communication and integration between the right and left hemispheres of the brain, leading to a more holistic and integrated understanding and processing of these experiences. Psychodrama may stimulate neural pathways that allow for a deeper exploration and synthesis of both the emotional and cognitive aspects of past experiences.

A recent preliminary study by Lim et al. (2024) used functional Near-Infrared Spectroscopy (fNIRS)[24] to examine the neurophysiological mechanisms of the role-reversal technique. They found that during dyadic role-play (where participants took on the roles of two mutual friends), there was reduced brain activity in the front left part of the prefrontal cortex associated with self-reflection compared to when participants engaged in naturalistic conversation and acted as themselves. This suggests that in psychodrama, where individuals assume roles and seek to understand others' perspectives (i.e., perspective-taking), they focus less on themselves, which aligns with the socio-cognitive function of the role-reversal technique.

7.5.2 Relational Neuroaesthetics

Neuroaesthetics is an interdisciplinary field that explores the neural bases of aesthetic experiences, and focuses on the perception, appreciation, and, to a lesser extent, creation of art and aesthetics (Chatterjee & Cardilo, 2021). Mounting evidence suggests that an aesthetic experience emerges from the dynamic interaction between distributed neural systems by activating various perceptual, cognitive, and emotional brain functions (Skov & Nadal, 2022). An aesthetic experience arises dynamically from the complex interplay of factors related to the perceived object (artwork, a piece of music, poetry, body movement, etc.), the individual's subjective response, and the situational context or setting within which the experience emerged (Jacobsen, 2006). Aesthetic experiences are inherently embodied (Casale et al., 2024), such that an external aesthetic object (e.g., auxiliary ego) triggers the observer's (e.g., the

---

[23] The limbic system consists of several interconnected structures, including the hippocampus, amygdala, thalamus, hypothalamus, basal ganglia, and cingulate gyrus.

[24] fNIRS is a non-invasive neuroimaging technique used to measure changes in brain activity by monitoring blood oxygenation levels in the brain.

protagonist's or the audience's) *mirroring mechanism* that elicits emotions, bodily memories, and imaginative associations that do not only shape their aesthetic experience but also have significant therapeutic potential (Vaisvaser et al., 2024; Yaniv, 2011). Thus, embodied aesthetics promote a brain-body-mind connection that integrates the action observation and sensorimotor systems in the brain, which are activated during both receptive and active artistic engagement via emotional and cognitive processing (Scarinzi, 2015; Vaisvaser et al., 2024).

In terms of *interpersonal neural synchrony*, studies have pointed to the potential of exploring how interactive real-world aesthetic experiences induce interpersonal brain-to-brain coupling, which refers to instances when the neural activity of two or more individuals becomes synchronized during social interactions (Vaisvaser et al., 2024). This synchronization is associated with a good client-therapist bond (Zhang et al., 2018) and feelings of shared intentionality, positive beliefs in cooperativity, and perceived social closeness in a group (Dikker et al., 2017). It should be noted that brain-to-brain synchrony is not a mechanism in itself but a measurable indicator of the neural dynamics underlying a relational psychological process (Dikker et al., 2017).

It has been suggested that "updating the prediction models of the brain may be the mechanism underlying psychotherapeutic changes" (Lin et al., 2023, p. 1077). The *predictive processing* framework of brain function suggests that the brain generates probabilistic models (predictors or "priors") to interpret sensory inputs and their causes, maintains balance through allostasis by minimizing prediction error, and anticipates and prepares for future events (Clark, 2013). Prediction errors (i.e., deviations from prior expectations) can generate surprise or uncertainty that triggers emotional or cognitive distress. This process guides the updating of predictions (priors) that are based on past experience by minimizing the "free energy"[25] associated with the difference between what the brain expects (predicted sensory inputs) and what it actually experiences (actual sensory inputs). In this sense, clients' problems can be seen as priors that do not update (Hauke & Lohr, 2022). Research indicates that a prediction error prompts the brain to update its current predictions to better align with the unexpected signals, which can result in modifying internal models and even reconsolidating traumatic memories destabilized because of the prediction error (Milton et al., 2023).

In the safe and structured psychodrama setting, sufficiently spontaneous protagonists operate within an unpredictable zone. A discrepancy between

---

[25] A theoretical construct borrowed from thermodynamics, "free energy" refers to the discrepancy between what the brain expects and what it actually experiences. It is defined as the energy that is available or "free" to be minimized by the brain's predictive mechanisms (Hauke & Lohr, 2022).

external stimuli (e.g., a corrective experience scene, a double offered or role-played by an auxiliary) and internal expectations (predictions) can result in a prediction error. By acknowledging and addressing the prediction error, protagonists can update their maladaptive internal predictive models. This process allows them to develop more adaptive coping strategies for future interactions, especially during triggering moments. These new strategies aim to replace maladaptive automatic thoughts or emotional/behavioral reactions, fixed habits, and distorted perceptions of self or others, as well as restructure the connections between distressing memories and current experiences.

To illustrate, imagine the case of Dan, whose childhood experiences shaped his brain's predictive mechanisms, leading to the development of deep-seated insecurities and mistrust in intimate relationships. Based on past experiences witnessing his parents' tumultuous relationship, Dan's brain predicts that future relationships will also be characterized by conflict and betrayal. These predictions create a heightened sensitivity to signs of potential abandonment or infidelity in his current relationship with Lea.

With the support of a containing double to regulate his emotional arousal, Dan revisits pivotal moments from his past and examines how these experiences have contributed to his current patterns of mistrust and fear of separation. In fact, Dan explores how his brain's predictive processes shape his perceptions and behaviors in relationships. By gaining insights into the origins of his insecurities, Dan begins to challenge and revise his brain's predictive models of relationships. With the guidance of his psychodramatist, Dan learns to recognize when his brain's predictions are based on past experiences rather than current reality. He develops strategies to regulate his emotional responses and effectively communicate his fears and insecurities with Lea. Over time, Dan's brain adapts its predictive mechanisms in response to the new constructive experiences, thus reducing his mistrust and separation fear and creating a more secure attachment style in his relationship with Lea.

Overall, combining psychophysiological and neurobiological indices can provide a more comprehensive understanding of processes and outcomes. Psychodrama researchers should consider using Mobile Brain-Body Imaging to capture real-time neural and physiological responses during sessions, which can offer insights into the embodied processes of therapeutic interactions (King & Parada, 2021; Vaisvaser et al., 2024). Researchers are encouraged to examine experiential approaches such as imagery-based treatment, which evokes emotional states, enhances emotion regulation, and influences the emotional impact of memories (Blackwell, 2019). Studies on mental imagery, such as imagery rescripting, can improve the design of psychodrama studies and help understand psychophysiological and neurobiological mechanisms of change (Çili & Stopa,

2021; Ji et al., 2017; Prinz et al., 2022; Skottnik & Linden, 2019). Collaboration with other arts therapies researchers can also provide valuable insights for psychodrama research (Kang et al., 2023; Malhotra et al., 2024; Vaisvaser, 2021).

7.6 Concluding Thoughts about Training

Psychotherapy researchers have recently recommended using automatically measured interpersonal synchrony in various modalities, such as text, audio, video, physiology, and neurology (Atzil-Slonim et al., 2023). Psychodrama students can benefit from learning to identify moments of increased and decreased synchrony, dys-synchrony, and avoidance in their responses and explore the context and consequences of these dynamics. They should learn to use their emotional arousal cues in response to the protagonist, recognize unhelpful synchronizations, and learn to down-regulate unproductive emotions while up-regulating productive ones. Another focus should be on understanding how external aesthetic objects (e.g., psychodramatic images, auxiliary egos) trigger emotional and bodily responses. Students should also learn to identify and use prediction errors as therapeutic opportunities, where they can help protagonists navigate unpredictable zones and update maladaptive predictive models. Practical exercises involving role-play and the doubling and mirroring techniques can help students learn how to prompt prediction errors and facilitate the protagonist's recognition and updating of predictive models. Incorporating these suggestions into training programs can help future psychodramatists better understand and apply cutting-edge knowledge and practices, thus ultimately strengthening psychodrama as a credible and thriving profession.

References

Abu Elheja, R., Palgi, Y., Feldman, R. et al. (2021). The role of oxytocin in regulating loneliness in old age. *Psychoneuroendocrinology*, *133*, 105413. https://doi.org/10.1016/j.psyneuen.2021.105413.

Alarcon, G. M., Bowling, N. A., & Khazon, S. (2013). Great expectations: A meta-analytic examination of optimism and hope. *Personality and Individual Differences*, *54*(7), 821–827. https://doi.org/10.1016/j.paid.2012.12.004.

Altmann, U., Schoenherr, D., Paulick, J. et al. (2020). Associations between movement synchrony and outcome in patients with social anxiety disorder: Evidence for treatment specific effects. *Psychotherapy Research*, *30*(5), 574–590. https://doi.org/10.1080/10503307.2019.1630779.

Ang, K., Hepgul, N., Gao, W., & Higginson, I. J. (2018). Strategies used in improving and assessing the level of reporting of implementation fidelity in randomised controlled trials of palliative care complex interventions: A systematic review. *Palliative Medicine*, *32*(2), 500–516. https://doi.org/10.1177/0269216317717369.

Anthes, L. S., & Dreisoerner, A. (2024). Self-compassion and mental health: A systematic review and transactional model on mechanisms of change. *PsyArXiv Priprints*. https://doi.org/10.31234/osf.io/aucrz.

Appelbaum, M., Cooper, H., Kline, R. B. et al. (2018). Journal article reporting standards for quantitative research in psychology: The APA Publications and Communications Board task force report. *American Psychologist*, *73*(1), 3–25. https://doi.org/10.1037/amp0000191.

Arango, I., Miranda, E., Sánchez Ferrer, J. C. et al. (2019). Changes in facial emotion expression during a psychotherapeutic intervention for patients with borderline personality disorder. *Journal of Psychiatric Research*, *114*, 126–132. https://doi.org/10.1016/j.jpsychires.2019.04.026.

Aristotle, & Butcher, S. H. (1961). *Poetics*. Hill and Wang.

Atzil-Slonim, D. (2024). What are some primary future directions for psychotherapy research, practice, and training? In F. T. L. Leong, J. L. Callahan, J. Zimmerman, M. J. Constantino, & C. F. Eubanks (eds.), *APA handbook of psychotherapy: Evidence-based practice, practice-based evidence, and contextual participant-driven practice, Vol. 2* (pp. 323–338). American Psychological Association. https://doi.org/10.1037/0000354-021.

Atzil-Slonim, D., Soma, C. S., Zhang, X., Paz, A., & Imel, Z. E. (2023). Facilitating dyadic synchrony in psychotherapy sessions: Systematic review and meta-analysis. *Psychotherapy Research*, *33*(7), 898–917. https://doi.org/10.1080/10503307.2023.2191803.

Atzil-Slonim, D., Stolowicz-Melman, D., Bar-Kalifa, E. et al. (2022). Oxytocin reactivity to the therapeutic encounter as a biomarker of change in the treatment of depression. *Journal of Counseling Psychology*, *69*(5), 755–760. https://doi.org/10.1037/cou0000617.

Averill, J. R. (2005). Emotions as mediators and as products of creative activity. In J. Kaufman & J. Baer (eds.), *Creativity across domains: Faces of the muse* (pp. 225–243). Erlbaum.

Averill, J. R., Chon, K. K., & Hahn, D. W. (2001). Emotions and creativity, east and west. *Asian Journal of Social Psychology*, *4*(3), 165–183. https://doi.org/10.1111/1467-839X.00084.

Azoulay, B., & Orkibi, H. (2015). The four-phase CBN Psychodrama model: A manualized approach for practice and research. *The Arts in Psychotherapy*, *42*, 10–18. https://doi.org/10.1016/j.aip.2014.12.012.

Bachorowski, J.-A., & Owren, M. J. (2008). Vocal expressions of emotion. In M. Lewis, J. M. Haviland-Jones, & L. F. Barrett (eds.), *Handbook of emotions, 3rd ed.* (pp. 196–210). The Guilford Press.

Baker, F. A. (2022). *Leadership and management of clinical trials in creative arts therapy*. Springer.

Baker, F. A., Silverman, M. J., & MacDonald, R. (2016). Reliability and validity of the Meaningfulness of Songwriting Scale (MSS) with adults on acute psychiatric and detoxification units. *Journal of Music Therapy*, *53*(1), 55–74. https://doi.org/10.1093/jmt/thv020.

Bannister, A. (2007). Psychodrama and child development: Working with children. In C. Baim, J. Burmeister, & M. Maciel (eds.), *Psychodrama: Advances in theory and practice* (pp. 239–246). Routledge.

Bar-Kalifa, E., Prinz, J. N., Atzil-Slonim, D. et al. (2019). Physiological synchrony and therapeutic alliance in an imagery-based treatment. *Journal of Counseling Psychology*, *66*(4), 508–517. https://doi.org/10.1037/cou0000358.

Barnett, L. A. (2007). The nature of playfulness in young adults. *Personality and Individual Differences*, *43*(4), 949–958. https://doi.org/10.1016/j.paid.2007.02.018.

Bat Or, M., & Zilcha-Mano, S. (2019). The art therapy working alliance inventory: The development of a measure. *International Journal of Art Therapy*, *24*(2), 76–87. https://doi.org/10.1080/17454832.2018.1518989.

Bell, T., Montague, J., Elander, J., & Gilbert, P. (2020). "A definite feel-it moment": Embodiment, externalisation and emotion during chair-work in compassion-focused therapy. *Counselling and Psychotherapy Research*, *20* (1), 143–153. https://doi.org/10.1002/capr.12248.

Bellg, A. J., Borrelli, B., Resnick, B. et al. (2004). Enhancing treatment fidelity in health behavior change studies: Best practices and recommendations from the NIH Behavior Change Consortium. *Health Psychol*, *23*(5), 443–451. https://doi.org/10.1037/0278-6133.23.5.443.

Ben-Tzur, B., & Feniger-Schaal, R. (2025). Aesthetic distance: Conceptualization and practical use. *The Arts in Psychotherapy*, *92*, 102230. https://doi.org/10.1016/j.aip.2024.102230.

Biancalani, G., & Orkibi, H. (2025). Development and initial validation of the state spontaneity scale. *Psychology of Aesthetics, Creativity, and the Arts*, 1–17. Advance online publication. https://doi.org/10.1037/aca0000752.

Bilik, E. (2019). Neuropsychodrama: What is happening in our brains in psychodrama? *Revista Brasileira de Psicodrama*, *27*(2), 165–173.

Blackwell, S. E. (2019). Mental imagery: From basic research to clinical practice. *Journal of Psychotherapy Integration*, *29*(3), 235–247. https://doi.org/10.1037/int0000108.

Blatner, A. (1991). Role dynamics: A comprehensive theory of psychology. *Journal of Group Psychotherapy, Psychodrama & Sociometry*, *44*(1), 33–40.

Blatner, A. (1996). *Acting-in: Practical applications of psychodramatic methods* (3rd ed.). Springer.

Blatner, A. (2000a). *Foundations of psychodrama: History, theory, and practice* (4th ed.). Springer.

Blatner, A. (2000b). Psychodramatic methods for facilitating bereavement. In P. F. Kellerman & M. K. Hudgins (eds.), *Psychodrama with trauma survivors: Acting out your pain* (pp. 41-50). Jessica Kingsley.

Blatner, A. (2006). The choosing self: Developing the meta-role functions. www.blatner.com/adam/psyntbk/choosingself.html.

Blatner, A., & Cukier, R. (2007). Appendix: Moreno's basic concepts. In C. Baim, J. Burmeister, & M. Maciel (eds.), *Psychodrama: Advances in theory and practice* (pp. 293–306). Routledge.

Boria, G. (1989). Conceptual clarity in psychodrama training. *Journal of group psychotherapy, psychodrama and sociometry*, *42*(3), 166–172.

Braun, V., & Clarke, V. (2021). *Thematic analysis: A practical guide*. SAGE.

Bryant, A., & Charmaz, K. (2007). *The Sage handbook of grounded theory*. SAGE.

Buchanan, D. R. (1984). Moreno's social atom: A diagnostic and treatment tool for exploring interpersonal relationships. *The Arts in Psychotherapy*, *11*(3), 155–164. https://doi.org/10.1016/0197-4556(84)90035-2.

Buchanan, G. M., & Seligman, M. E. P. (1995). *Explanatory style*. Routledge.

Bucuță, M. D., Dima, G., & Testoni, I. (2018). "When you thought that there is no one and nothing": The value of psychodrama in working with abused women. *Frontiers in Psychology*, *9*(1518), 1–16. https://doi.org/10.3389/fpsyg.2018.01518.

Bustos, D. M. (1994). Locus, matrix, status nascendi and the concept of clusters. In P. Holmes, M. Karp, & M. Watson (eds.), *Psychodrama since Moreno: Innovations in theory and practice* (pp. 45–55). Routledge.

Butcher, N. J., Monsour, A., Mew, E. J. et al. (2022). Guidelines for reporting outcomes in trial reports: The CONSORT-Outcomes 2022 Extension. *JAMA*, *328*(22), 2252–2264. https://doi.org/10.1001/jama.2022.21022.

Callero, P. (1994). From role-playing to role-using: Understanding role as resource. *Social Psychology Quarterly*, *57*(3), 228–243.

Carey, T. A., Griffiths, R., Dixon, J. E., & Hines, S. (2020). Identifying functional mechanisms in psychotherapy: A scoping systematic review. *Frontiers in Psychiatry*, *11*, 1–9. https://doi.org/10.3389/fpsyt.2020.00291.

Carr, A., Cullen, K., Keeney, C. et al. (2021). Effectiveness of positive psychology interventions: a systematic review and meta-analysis. *The Journal of Positive Psychology*, *16*(6), 749–769. https://doi.org/10.1080/17439760.2020.1818807.

Carr, A., Finneran, L., Boyd, C. et al. (2024). The evidence-base for positive psychology interventions: a mega-analysis of meta-analyses. *The Journal of Positive Psychology*, *19*(2), 191–205. https://doi.org/10.1080/17439760.2023.2168564.

Carroll, C., Patterson, M., Wood, S. et al. (2007). A conceptual framework for implementation fidelity. *Implementation Science*, *2*(1), 1–9, Article 40. https://doi.org/10.1186/1748-5908-2-40.

Carroll, K. M., Martino, S., & Rounsaville, B. J. (2010). No train, no gain? *Clinical Psychology: Science and Practice*, *17*(1), 36–40. https://doi.org/10.1111/j.1468-2850.2009.01190.x.

Carroll, L. (1971/1865). *Alice in wonderland*. W. W. Norton.

Casale, C., Moffat, R., & Cross, E. S. (2024). Aesthetic evaluation of body movements shaped by embodiment and arts experience: Insights from behaviour and fNIRS. *Scientific Reports*, *14*(1), 25841. https://doi.org/10.1038/s41598-024-75427-9.

Casson, J. (1997). Dramatherapy history in headlines: Who did what, when, where? *Dramatherapy*, *19*(2), 10–13. https://doi.org/10.1080/02630672.1997.9689446.

Casson, J. (2006). Shakespeare and the healing drama. *Dramatherapy*, *28*(1), 18–20. https://doi.org/10.1080/02630672.2006.9689683.

Casson, J. (2007a). 17th century theatre therapy. *Dramatherapy*, *29*(1), 3–9. https://doi.org/10.1080/02630672.2008.9689731.

Casson, J. (2007b). The Sun's Darling: A sixth Jacobean healing drama. *Dramatherapy*, *29*(2), 17–17. https://doi.org/10.1080/02630672.2007.9689721.

Casson, J. (2016). Shamanism, theatre and dramatherapy. In S. Jennings & C. Holmwood (eds.), *Routledge international handbook of dramatherapy* (pp. 125–134). Routledge.

Castonguay, L. G., Boswell, J. F., Zack, S. E. et al. (2010). Helpful and hindering events in psychotherapy: A practice research network study. *Psychotherapy: Theory, Research, Practice, Training*, *47*(3), 327–344. https://doi.org/10.1037/a0021164.

Chatterjee, A., & Cardilo, E. (eds.). (2021). *Brain, beauty, and art: Essays bringing neuroaesthetics into focus*. Oxford University Press. https://doi.org/10.1093/oso/9780197513620.001.0001.

Christoforou, A., & Kipper, D. A. (2006). The spontaneity assessment inventory (SAI), anxiety, obsessive-compulsive tendency, and temporal orientation. *Journal of Group Psychotherapy, Psychodrama & Sociometry*, *59*(1), 23–34.

Chu, P. S., Saucier, D. A., & Hafner, E. (2010). Meta-analysis of the relationships between social support and well-being in children and adolescents. *Journal of Social and Clinical Psychology*, *29*(6), 624–645. https://doi.org/10.1521/jscp.2010.29.6.624.

Çili, S., & Stopa, L. (2021). A narrative identity perspective on mechanisms of change in imagery rescripting. *Frontiers in Psychiatry*, *12*, 1–5. https://doi.org/10.3389/fpsyt.2021.636071.

Clark, A. (2013). Whatever next? Predictive brains, situated agents, and the future of cognitive science. *Behavioral and Brain Sciences*, *36*(3), 181–204. https://doi.org/10.1017/S0140525X12000477.

Clayton, G. M. (1994). Role theory and its application in clinical practice. In P. Holmes, M. Karp, & M. Watson (eds.), *Psychodrama since Moreno: Innovations in theory and practice* (pp. 86–105). Routledge.

Cohen, K., Ramseyer, F. T., Tal, S., & Zilcha-Mano, S. (2021). Nonverbal synchrony and the alliance in psychotherapy for major depression: Disentangling state-like and trait-like effects. *Clinical Psychological Science*, *9*(4), 634–648. https://doi.org/10.1177/2167702620985294.

Cohen, S., Gottlieb, B., & Underwood, L. (2000). Social relationships and health. In S. Cohen, L. Underwood, & B. Gottlieb (eds.), *Social support measurement and intervention: A guide for health and social scientists* (pp. 3–25). Oxford University Press.

Cohen, S., & Wills, T. A. (1985). Stress, social support, and the buffering hypothesis. *Psychological Bulletin*, *98*(2), 310–357. https://doi.org/10.1037/0033-2909.98.2.310.

Cowand, A., Amarsaikhan, U., Ricks, R. F., Cash, E. D., & Sephton, S. E. (2024). Self-compassion is associated with improved well-being and healthier cortisol profiles in undergraduate students. *Mindfulness*, *15*(7), 1831–1845. https://doi.org/10.1007/s12671-024-02383-w.

Cozolino, L. J. (2014). *The neuroscience of human relationships: Attachment and the developing social brain* (2nd ed.). W.W. Norton.

Crits-Christoph, P., Connolly Gibbons, M. B., & Mukherjee, D. (2013). Psychotherapy process-outcome research. In M. J. Lambert (ed.), *Bergin and Garfield's handbook of psychotherapy and behavior change* (6th ed., pp. 298–340). John Wiley & Sons.

Cruz, A., Sales, C. M. D., Alves, P., & Moita, G. (2018). The core techniques of Morenian psychodrama: A systematic review of literature. *Frontiers in Psychology*, *9*, 1–11. https://doi.org/10.3389/fpsyg.2018.01263.

Cruz, A. S., Dias Sales, C. M., Moita, G., & Alves, P. G. (2016). Towards the development of Helpful Aspects of Morenian Psychodrama Content Analysis System (HAMPCAS). In C. Stadler, M. Wieser, & K. Kirk (eds.), *Psychodrama: Empirical research and science 2* (pp. 57–67). Springer Fachmedien Wiesbaden. https://doi.org/10.1007/978-3-658-13015-2_6.

Csikszentmihalyi, M. (1991). *Flow: The psychology of optimal experience*. HarperPerennial.

Davis, M. H. (1983). Measuring individual differences in empathy: Evidence for a multidimensional approach. *Journal of Personality and Social Psychology*, *44*(1), 113–126. https://doi.org/10.1037/0022-3514.44.1.113.

Dayton, T. (1990). *Drama games: Techniques for self-development*. Health Communications.

Dayton, T. (2005). *The living stage: A step-by-step guide to psychodrama, sociometry, and experiential group therapy*. Health Communications.

Dayton, T. (2016). Neuropsychodrama in the treatment of relational trauma: Relational trauma repair—An experiential model for treating posttraumatic stress disorder. *The Journal of Psychodrama, Sociometry, and Group Psychotherapy*, *64*(1), 41–50.

de Felice, G., Giuliani, A., Halfon, S. et al. (2019). The misleading Dodo Bird verdict. How much of the outcome variance is explained by common and specific factors? *New Ideas in Psychology*, *54*, 50–55. https://doi.org/10.1016/j.newideapsych.2019.01.006.

de Witte, M., Orkibi, H., Zarate, R. et al. (2021). From therapeutic factors to mechanisms of change in the creative arts therapies: A scoping review.

Frontiers in Psychology, 12(2525), 1–27. https://doi.org/10.3389/fpsyg.2021.678397.

Deits-Lebehn, C., Baucom, K. J. W., Crenshaw, A. O., Smith, T. W., & Baucom, B. R. W. (2020). Incorporating physiology into the study of psychotherapy process. *Journal of Counseling Psychology, 67*(4), 488–499. https://doi.org/10.1037/cou0000391.

Denton, W. H., Johnson, S. M., & Burleson, B. R. (2009). Emotion focused therapy-therapist fidelity scale (EFT-TFS): Conceptual development and content validity. *Journal of Couple & Relationship Therapy, 8*(3), 226–246. https://doi.org/10.1080/15332690903048820.

DeRobertis, E. M., & Bland, A. M. (2021). Humanistic and positive psychologies: The continuing narrative after two decades. *Journal of Humanistic Psychology*, 1–33. Advance online publication. https://doi.org/10.1177/00221678211008353.

Di Bello, M., Carnevali, L., Petrocchi, N. et al. (2020). The compassionate vagus: A meta-analysis on the connection between compassion and heart rate variability. *Neuroscience & Biobehavioral Reviews, 116*, 21–30. https://doi.org/10.1016/j.neubiorev.2020.06.016.

Dikker, S., Wan, L., Davidesco, I. et al. (2017). Brain-to-brain synchrony tracks real-world dynamic group interactions in the classroom. *Current Biology, 27*(9), 1375–1380. https://doi.org/10.1016/j.cub.2017.04.002.

dos Santos, F. R. M., Bazán, P. R., Balardin, J. B. et al. (2022). Changes in prefrontal fNIRS activation and heart rate variability during self-compassionate thinking related to stressful memories. *Mindfulness, 13*(2), 326–338. https://doi.org/10.1007/s12671-021-01789-0.

Dwan, K., Li, T., Altman, D. G., & Elbourne, D. (2019). CONSORT 2010 statement: Extension to randomised crossover trials. *BMJ, 366*, l4378. https://doi.org/10.1136/bmj.l4378.

Eldridge, S. M., Chan, C. L., Campbell, M. J. et al. (2016). CONSORT 2010 statement: extension to randomised pilot and feasibility trials. *BMJ, 355*, i5239. https://doi.org/10.1136/bmj.i5239.

Eliade, M. (1972). *Shamanism: Archaic techniques of ecstasy*. Princeton University Press.

Elkarif, T., Orkibi, H., & Keisari, S. (2024). Tele-drama therapy for community dwelling older adults with constricted life-space mobility: A randomized controlled trial. *The Journal of Positive Psychology*, 1–16. Advance online publication. https://doi.org/10.1080/17439760.2024.2427581.

Elliott, R. (2010). Psychotherapy change process research: Realizing the promise. *Psychotherapy Research, 20*(2), 123–135. https://doi.org/10.1080/10503300903470743.

Elliott, R. (2012). Qualitative methods for studying psychotherapy change processes. In D. Harper & A. R. Thompson (eds.), *Qualitative research methods in mental health and psychotherapy* (pp. 69–81). Wiley https://doi.org/10.1002/9781119973249.ch6.

Elliott, R., Greenberg, L. S., Watson, J. C., Timulak, L., & Freire, E. (2013). Research on humanistic-experiential psychotherapies. In M. J. Lambert (ed.), *Bergin & Garfield's handbook of psychotherapy and behavior change* (6th ed., pp. 495–538). Wiley.

Elliott, R., James, E., Reimschuessel, C., Cislo, D., & Sack, N. (1985). Significant events and the analysis of immediate therapeutic impacts. *Psychotherapy: Theory, Research, Practice, Training*, *22*(3), 620–630. https://doi.org/10.1037/h0085548.

Elliott, R., & Rodgers, B. (2008). *Client change interview schedule (v5)*. www.drbrianrodgers.com/research/client-change-interview.

Elliott, R., & Shapiro, D. A. (1988). Brief structured recall: A more efficient method for studying significant therapy events. *British Journal of Medical Psychology*, *61*(2), 141–153. https://doi.org/10.1111/j.2044-8341.1988.tb02773.x.

Elliott, R., Watson, J. C., Goldman, R. N., & Greenberg, L. S. (2004a). Empty chair work for unfinished interpersonal issues. In *Learning emotion-focused therapy: The process-experiential approach to change* (pp. 243–265). American Psychological Association. https://doi.org/10.1037/10725-012.

Elliott, R., Watson, J. C., Goldman, R. N., & Greenberg, L. S. (2004b). Two-chair work for conflict splits. In *Learning emotion-focused therapy: The process-experiential approach to change* (pp. 219–241). American Psychological Association. https://doi.org/10.1037/10725-011.

Emmons, R. A. (2013). *Gratitude works! A twenty-one-day program for creating emotional prosperity*. Jossey-Bass.

Emunah, R., & Johnson, D. R. (2009). *Current approaches in drama therapy* (2 ed.). C. C. Thomas.

Feldman, D. B., Rand, K. L., & Kahle-Wrobleski, K. (2009). Hope and goal attainment: Testing a basic prediction of hope theory. *Journal of Social and Clinical Psychology*, *28*(4), 479–497. https://doi.org/10.1521/jscp.2009.28.4.479.

Feniger-Schaal, R., Constien, T., & Orkibi, H. (2024). Playfulness in times of extreme adverse conditions: A theoretical model and case illustrations. *Humanities and Social Sciences Communications*, *11*(1), 1446. https://doi.org/10.1057/s41599-024-03936-z.

Feniger-Schaal, R., & Orkibi, H. (2020). Integrative systematic review of drama therapy intervention research. *Psychology of Aesthetics, Creativity, and the Arts, 14*(1), 68–80. https://doi.org/10.1037/aca0000257.

Fischer, S., & Zilcha-Mano, S. (2022). Why does psychotherapy work and for whom? Hormonal answers. *Biomedicines, 10*(6), 1361. www.mdpi.com/2227-9059/10/6/1361.

Fisher, H., Reiss, P. T., Atias, D. et al. (2023). Facing emotions: Between- and within-sessions changes in facial expression during psychological treatment for depression. *Clinical Psychological Science*, 1–15. https://doi.org/10.1177/21677026231195793.

Fleury, H. J., Marra, M. M., & Hadler, O. H. (2022). *Psychodrama in Brazil: Contemporary applications in mental health, education, and communities.* Springer.

Forsyth, D. R. (2015). Group psychotherapy, clinical psychology of. In J. D. Wright (ed.), *International encyclopedia of the social & behavioral sciences (2nd ed.)* (pp. 428–433). Elsevier. https://doi.org/10.1016/B978-0-08-097086-8.21066-0.

Frahsek, S., Mack, W., Mack, C., Pfalz-Blezinger, C., & Knopf, M. (2010). Assessing different aspects of pretend play within a play setting: Towards a standardized assessment of pretend play in young children. *British Journal of Developmental Psychology, 28*(2), 331–345. https://doi.org/10.1348/026151009X413666.

Frazier, P. A., Tix, A. P., & Barron, K. E. (2004). Testing moderator and mediator effects in counseling psychology research. *Journal of Counseling Psychology, 51*, 115–134. https://doi.org/10.1037/0022-0167.51.1.115.

Frydman, J. S., Cook, A., Armstrong, C. R., Rowe, C., & Kern, C. (2022). The drama therapy core processes: A Delphi study establishing a North American perspective. *The Arts in Psychotherapy, 80*, 101939. https://doi.org/10.1016/j.aip.2022.101939.

Gable, S. L., & Reis, H. T. (2010). Good news! Capitalizing on positive events in an interpersonal context. In P. Z. Mark (ed.), *Advances in experimental social psychology* (Vol. 42, pp. 195–257). Elsevier Press. https://doi.org/10.1016/S0065-2601(10)42004-3.

Gable, S. L., Reis, H. T., Impett, E. A., & Asher, E. R. (2004). What do you do when things go right? The intrapersonal and interpersonal benefits of sharing positive events. *Journal of Personality and Social Psychology, 87*(2), 228–245. https://doi.org/10.1037/0022-3514.87.2.228.

Garcia, A., & Buchanan, D. R. (2009). Psychodrama. In D. R. Johnson & R. Emunah (eds.), *Current approaches in drama therapy* (2 ed., pp. 393–423). Charles C. Thomas.

Gatta, M., Lara, D. Z., Lara, D. C. et al. (2010). Analytical psychodrama with adolescents suffering from psycho-behavioral disorder: Short-term effects on psychiatric symptoms. *The Arts in Psychotherapy*, *37*(3), 240–247. https://doi.org/10.1016/j.aip.2010.04.010.

Gelo, O. C. G., Pritz, A., & Rieken, B. (2015). *Psychotherapy research: Foundations, process, and outcome*. Springer Vienna.

Gendlin, E. T. (1996). *Focusing-oriented psychotherapy: A manual of the experiential method*. Guilford Press.

Gernert, C. C., Nelson, A., Falkai, P., & Falter-Wagner, C. M. (2024). Synchrony in psychotherapy: High physiological positive concordance predicts symptom reduction and negative concordance predicts symptom aggravation. *International Journal of Methods in Psychiatric Research*, *33*(1), e1978. https://doi.org/10.1002/mpr.1978.

Giacomucci, S. (2021). *Social work, sociometry, and psychodrama: Experiential approaches for group therapists, community leaders, and social workers*. Springer Nature. https://doi.org/10.1007/978-981-33-6342-7.

Ginsburg, L. R., Hoben, M., Easterbrook, A. et al. (2021). Fidelity is not easy! Challenges and guidelines for assessing fidelity in complex interventions. *Trials*, *22*(1), 372. https://doi.org/10.1186/s13063-021-05322-5.

Glaser, B. (2004). Ancient traditions within a new drama therapy method: Shamanism and developmental transformations. *The Arts in Psychotherapy*, *31*(2), 77–88. https://doi.org/10.1016/j.aip.2004.02.001.

Goethe, J. W. (1788/1973). *Lila* (O. Danielsson, Trans.). Unpublished manuscript (Original work published 1788).

Goffman, E. (1973). *The presentation of self in everyday life*. Overlook Press.

Goldman, E. E., & Morrison, D. S. (1984). *Psychodrama: Experience and process*. Kendall.

Golland, Y., Ben-David, B., & Keisari, S. (2024). *Brains on playfulness: Playful interactions enhance cognition in older ages*. Paper presented at the 7th Biannual Conference of the European Society for Cognitive and Affective Neuroscience (ESCAN), Ghent, Belgium.

Golland, Y., Ben-David, B. M., Mather, M., & Keisari, S. (2025). Playful brains: A possible neurobiological pathway to cognitive health in aging. *Frontiers in Human Neuroscience*, *19*, 1–15. https://doi.org/10.3389/fnhum.2025.1490864.

Grawe, K. (1997). Research-informed psychotherapy. *Psychotherapy Research*, *7*(1), 1–19. https://doi.org/10.1080/10503309712331331843.

Greenberg, L. S. (1986). Change process research. *Journal of Consulting and Clinical Psychology*, *54*(1), 4–9. https://doi.org/10.1037/0022-006X.54.1.4.

Gupta, S. K. (2011). Intention-to-treat concept: A review. *Perspectives in Clinical Research*, *2*(3), 109–112. https://doi.org/10.4103/2229-3485.83221.

Hardy, G. E., & Llewelyn, S. (2015). Introduction to psychotherapy process research. In O. C. G. Gelo, A. Pritz, & B. Rieken (eds.), *Psychotherapy research: Foundations, process, and outcome* (pp. 183–194). Springer Vienna. https://doi.org/10.1007/978-3-7091-1382-0_9.

Hare, A. P., & Hare, J. R. (1996). *J. L. Moreno*. SAGE.

Harms, E. (1957). Modern Psychotherapy – 150 years ago. *Journal of Mental Science*, *103*(433), 804–809.

Harris, P. L. (2000). *The work of the imagination*. Blackwell.

Hauke, G., & Lohr, C. (2022). Piloting the update: The use of therapeutic relationship for change – a free energy account. *Frontiers in Psychology*, *13*, 1–15. https://doi.org/10.3389/fpsyg.2022.842488.

Hayes, A. F. (2013). *Introduction to mediation, moderation, and conditional process analysis: A regression-based approach*. Guilford Press.

Hayes, A. M., Laurenceau, J.-P., & Cardaciotto, L. (2008). Methods for capturing the process of change. In A. M. Nezu & C. M. Nezu (eds.), *Evidence-based outcome research: A practical guide to conducting randomized controlled trials for psychosocial interventions* (pp. 335–358). Oxford University Press.

Heppner, P. P., Wampold, B. E., Owen, J., Wang, K. T., & Thompson, M. N. (2015). *Research design in counseling* (4th ed.). Cengage Learning.

Herriot, H., Wrosch, C., & Gouin, J.-P. (2018). Self-compassion, chronic age-related stressors, and diurnal cortisol secretion in older adulthood. *Journal of Behavioral Medicine*, *41*(6), 850–862. https://doi.org/10.1007/s10865-018-9943-6.

Hildebrand, M. W., Host, H. H., Binder, E. F. et al. (2012). Measuring treatment fidelity in a rehabilitation intervention study. *American Journal of Physical Medicine & Rehabilitation*, *91*(8), 715–724. https://doi.org/10.1097/PHM.0b013e31824ad462.

Hoffmann, T. C., Glasziou, P. P., Boutron, I. et al. (2014). Better reporting of interventions: template for intervention description and replication (TIDieR) checklist and guide. *BMJ*, *348*, g1687. https://doi.org/10.1136/bmj.g1687.

Hollander, C. E. (2002). A process for psychodrama training: The Hollander psychodrama curve. *International Journal of Action Methods*, *54*(4), 147–157.

Horvath, A. O., & Greenberg, L. S. (1989). Development and validation of the working alliance inventory. *Journal of Counseling Psychology*, *36*(2), 223–233. https://doi.org/10.1037/0022-0167.36.2.223.

Huber, J., Jennissen, S., Nikendei, C., Schauenburg, H., & Dinger, U. (2021). Agency and alliance as change factors in psychotherapy. *Journal of Consulting and Clinical Psychology*, *89*(3), 214–226. https://doi.org/10.1037/ccp0000628.

Hudgins, K., & Toscani, F. (2014). Containment = Safety with Action Methods. *The Journal of Psychodrama, Sociometry, and Group Psychotherapy*, *62*(1), 105–110. https://doi.org/10.12926/0731-1273-62.1.105.

Hudgins, M. K., & Drucker, K. (1998). The containing double as part of the therapeutic spiral model for treating trauma survivors. *International Journal of Action Methods*, *51*, 63–74.

Hug, E. (2007). A neuroscience perspective on psychodrama. In C. Baim, J. Burmeister, & M. Maciel (eds.), *Psychodrama: Advances in theory and practice* (pp. 227–238). Routledge.

Hug, E. (2013). A Neuroscience perspective on trauma and action methods. In K. Hudgins & F. Toscani (eds.), *Healing world trauma with the therapeutic spiral model* (pp. 111–131). Jessica Kingsley.

Huizinga, J. (1944). *Homo Ludens: A study of the play-element in culture*. Routledge & Kegan Paul.

Imel, Z. E., Barco, J. S., Brown, H. J. et al. (2014). The association of therapist empathy and synchrony in vocally encoded arousal. *Journal of Counseling Psychology*, *61*(1), 146–153. https://doi.org/10.1037/a0034943.

Imus, S. D. (2021). Creating breeds creating. In H. Wengrower & S. Chaiklin (eds.), *Dance and creativity within dance movement therapy: International perspectives* (pp. 124–140). Routledge. https://doi.org/10.4324/9780429442308.

Jacobsen, T. (2006). Bridging the arts and sciences: A framework for the psychology of aesthetics. *Leonardo*, *39*(2), 155–162. https://doi.org/10.1162/leon.2006.39.2.155.

Jans-Beken, L., Jacobs, N., Janssens, M. et al. (2020). Gratitude and health: An updated review. *The Journal of Positive Psychology*, *15*(6), 743–782. https://doi.org/10.1080/17439760.2019.1651888.

Jarlais, D. C. D., Lyles, C., Crepaz, N., & Group, t. T. (2004). Improving the reporting quality of nonrandomized evaluations of behavioral and public health interventions: The TREND statement. *American Journal of Public Health*, *94*(3), 361–366. https://doi.org/10.2105/ajph.94.3.361.

Jennings, S. (1995). *Theatre, ritual, and transformation: The Senoi Temiars*. Routledge.

Ji, J. L., Holmes, E. A., & Blackwell, S. E. (2017). Seeing light at the end of the tunnel: Positive prospective mental imagery and optimism in depression. *Psychiatry research, 247,* 155–162. https://doi.org/10.1016/j.psychres.2016.11.025.

Johnson, D. R. (1998). On the therapeutic action of the creative arts therapies: The psychodynamic model. *The Arts in Psychotherapy, 25*(2), 85–99.

Jones, P. (2007). *Drama as therapy: Theory, practice, and research* (2nd ed.). Routledge.

Jones, P. (2021). *The arts therapies: A revolution in healthcare* (2nd ed.). Routledge.

Juszczak, E., Altman, D. G., Hopewell, S., & Schulz, K. (2019). Reporting of multi-arm parallel-group randomized trials: Extension of the CONSORT 2010 Statement. *JAMA, 321*(16), 1610–1620. https://doi.org/10.1001/jama.2019.3087.

Kang, K., Orlandi, S., Leung, J. et al. (2023). Electroencephalographic interbrain synchronization in children with disabilities, their parents, and neurologic music therapists. *European Journal of Neuroscience, 58*(1), 2367–2383. https://doi.org/10.1111/ejn.16036.

Kapitan, L. (2012). Does art therapy work? Identifying the active ingredients of art therapy efficacy. *Art Therapy, 29*(2), 48–49. https://doi.org/10.1080/07421656.2012.684292.

Kaufman, J. C., & Baer, J. (2012). Beyond new and appropriate: Who decides what is creative? *Creativity Research Journal, 24,* 83–91. https://doi.org/10.1080/10400419.2012.649237.

Kazdin, A. E. (2009). Understanding how and why psychotherapy leads to change. *Psychotherapy Research, 19*(4–5), 418–428. https://doi.org/10.1080/10503300802448899.

Kazdin, A. E. (2011). *Single-case research designs: Methods for clinical and applied settings* (2nd ed.). Oxford University Press.

Kazdin, A. E. (2014). Moderators, mediators and mechanisms of change in psychotherapy. In W. Lutz & S. Knox (eds.), *Quantitative and qualitative methods in psychotherapy research* (pp. 87–101). Routledge.

Kedem-Tahar, E., & Kellermann, P. F. (1996). Psychodrama and drama therapy: A comparison. *The Arts in Psychotherapy, 23*(1), 27–36. https://doi.org/10.1016/0197-4556(95)00059-3.

Keisari, S. (2021). Expanding the role repertoire while aging: A drama therapy model. *Frontiers in Psychology, 12,* 635975–635975. https://doi.org/10.3389/fpsyg.2021.635975.

Kellar, H., Treadwell, T. W., Kumar, V. K., & Leach, E. S. (2002). The personal attitude scale-II: A revised measure of spontaneity. *Journal of Group Psychotherapy, Psychodrama, & Sociometry, 55,* 35–46.

Kellermann, P. F. (1984). The place of catharsis in psychodrama. *Journal of Group Psychotherapy, Psychodrama and Sociometry*, *37*(1), 1–13.

Kellermann, P. F. (1985). Participants' perception of therapeutic factors in psychodrama. *Journal of Group Psychotherapy, Psychodrama & Sociometry*, *38*(3), 123–132.

Kellermann, P. F. (1987a). A proposed definition of psychodrama. *Journal of Group Psychotherapy, Psychodrama and Sociometry*, *40*(2), 76–80.

Kellermann, P. F. (1987b). Psychodrama participants' perception of therapeutic factors. *Small Group Research*, *18*(3), 408–419. https://doi.org/10.1177/104649648701800307.

Kellermann, P. F. (2000a). Action insight. In *Focus on psychodrama: The therapeutic aspects of psychodrama* (pp. 84–97). Jessica Kingsley.

Kellermann, P. F. (2000b). *Focus on psychodrama: The therapeutic aspects of psychodrama*. Jessica Kingsley.

Kellermann, P. F. (2007a). Let's face it: Mirroring in psychodrama. In C. Baim, J. Burmeister, & M. Maciel (eds.), *Psychodrama: Advances in theory and practice* (pp. 83–95). Routledge.

Kellermann, P. F. (2007b). *Sociodrama and collective trauma*. Jessica Kingsley.

Keyes, C. L. M. (2002). The mental health continuum: From languishing to flourishing in life. *Journal of Health and Social Behavior*, *43*(2), 207–222. www.jstor.org/stable/3090197.

Keyes, C. L. M. (2013). *Mental well-being: International contributions to the study of positive mental health*. Springer.

Kim, J. J., Sherwell, C., Parker, S. L., & Kirby, J. N. (2024). Compassion training influences heart-rate variability within severe depression. *Journal of Affective Disorders Reports*, *16*, 100760. https://doi.org/10.1016/j.jadr.2024.100760.

King, J. L., & Parada, F. J. (2021). Using mobile brain/body imaging to advance research in arts, health, and related therapeutics. *European Journal of Neuroscience*, *54*(12), 8364–8380. https://doi.org/10.1111/ejn.15313.

Kipper, D. A. (1986). *Psychotherapy through clinical role playing*. Brunner/Mazel.

Kipper, D. A., & Ben-Ely, Z. (1979). The effectiveness of the psychodramatic double method, the reflection method, and lecturing in the training of empathy. *Journal of Clinical Psychology*, *35*(2), 370–375. https://doi.org/10.1002/1097-4679(197904)35:2<370::aid-jclp2270350229>3.0.co;2-y.

Kipper, D. A., Green, D. J., & Prorak, A. (2010). The relationship among spontaneity, impulsivity, and creativity. *Journal of Creativity in Mental Health*, *5*(1), 39–53. https://doi.org/10.1080/15401381003640866.

Kipper, D. A., & Hundal, J. (2005). The spontaneity assessment inventory: The relationship between spontaneity and nonspontaneity. *Journal of Group Psychotherapy, Psychodrama, & Sociometry, 58*(3), 119–129.

Kipper, D. A., & Shemer, H. (2006). The revised spontaneity assessment inventory (SAI-R): Spontaneity, well-being, and stress. *Journal of Group Psychotherapy, Psychodrama, & Sociometry, 59*, 127–136.

Kirby, E. T. (1974). The shamanistic origins of popular entertainments. *The Drama Review: TDR, 18*(1), 5–15. https://doi.org/10.2307/1144856.

Kirby, J. N., Doty, J. R., Petrocchi, N., & Gilbert, P. (2017). The current and future role of heart rate variability for assessing and training compassion. *Frontiers in Public Health, 5*, 1–6. https://doi.org/10.3389/fpubh.2017.00040.

Knittel, M. G. (2009). *Counseling and drama: Psychodrama a deux*. Xlibris.

Koenig, H. G., Westlund, R. E., George, L. K. et al. (1993). Abbreviating the Duke Social Support Index for use in chronically ill elderly individuals. *Psychosomatics, 34*(1), 61–69. https://doi.org/10.1016/S0033-3182(93)71928-3.

Koole, S. L., & Tschacher, W. (2016). Synchrony in psychotherapy: A review and an integrative framework for the therapeutic alliance. *Frontiers in Psychology, 7*, 862–862. https://doi.org/10.3389/fpsyg.2016.00862.

Kratochwill, T. R., Hitchcock, J., Horner, R. et al. (2010). Single-case designs technical documentation. *What Works Clearinghouse*. https://ies.ed.gov/ncee/wwc/Document/229.

Krause, M. (2024). Lessons from ten years of psychotherapy process research. *Psychotherapy Research, 34*(3), 261–275. https://doi.org/10.1080/10503307.2023.2200151.

Kushnir, A., & Orkibi, H. (2021). Concretization as a mechanism of change in psychodrama: Procedures and benefits. *Frontiers in Psychology, 12*(176), 1–13. https://doi.org/10.3389/fpsyg.2021.633069.

Lahad, M. (2017). From victim to victor: The development of the BASIC PH model of coping and resiliency. *Traumatology, 23*(1), 27–34. https://doi.org/10.1037/trm0000105.

Lahad, M., Shacham, M., & Ayalon, O. (2013). *The BASIC PH model of coping and resiliency: Theory, research and cross-cultural application*. Jessica Kingsley.

Laird, K. T., Tanner-Smith, E. E., Russell, A. C., Hollon, S. D., & Walker, L. S. (2017). Comparative efficacy of psychological therapies for improving mental health and daily functioning in irritable bowel syndrome: A systematic review and meta-analysis. *Clinical Psychology Review, 51*, 142–152. https://doi.org/10.1016/j.cpr.2016.11.001.

Lambert, M. J. (ed.) (2013a). *Bergin and Garfield's handbook of psychotherapy and behavior change* (6th ed.). John Wiley.

Lambert, M. J. (2013b). The efficacy and effectiveness of psychotherapy. In M. J. Lambert (ed.), *Bergin and Garfield's handbook of psychotherapy and behavior change* (6th ed., pp. 169–218). John Wiley.

Lambert, N. M., Gwinn, A. M., Baumeister, R. F. et al. (2013). A boost of positive affect: The perks of sharing positive experiences. *Journal of Social and Personal Relationships*, *30*(1), 24–43. https://doi.org/10.1177/0265407512449400.

Landy, R. J. (1982). Training the drama therapist: A four-part model. *The Arts in Psychotherapy*, *9*(2), 91–99. https://doi.org/10.1016/0197-4556(82)90012-0.

Langer, S. K. (1953). *Feeling and form: A theory of art*. Charles Scribner's Sons.

Laukka, P. (2017). Vocal communication of emotion. In V. Zeigler-Hill & T. K. Shackelford (eds.), *Encyclopedia of personality and individual differences* (pp. 1–6). Springer. https://doi.org/10.1007/978-3-319-28099-8_562-1.

Lawrence, C. (2015). The caring observer: Creating self-compassion through psychodrama. *The Journal of Psychodrama, Sociometry, and Group Psychotherapy*, *63*(1), 65–72.

Leach, J. D. (2003). Psychodrama and justice: Training trial lawyers. In J. Gershoni (ed.), *Psychodrama in the 21st century: Clinical and educational applications* (pp. 249–264). Springer.

Lelkes, O. (2021). *Sustainable hedonism: A thriving life that does not cost the earth-written by orsolya lelkes*. Bristol University Press.

Levi, E., Peysachov, G., Admon, R., & Zilcha-Mano, S. (2024). Cortisol interdependence during psychotherapy in major depressive disorder. *Psychoneuroendocrinology*, *163*, 106983. https://doi.org/10.1016/j.psyneuen.2024.106983.

Lillard, A. S. (2017). Why do the children (pretend) play? *Trends in Cognitive Sciences*, *21*(11), 826–834. https://doi.org/10.1016/j.tics.2017.08.001.

Lim, C. Y., & In, J. (2021). Considerations for crossover design in clinical study. *Korean Journal Anesthesiol*, *74*(4), 293–299. https://doi.org/10.4097/kja.21165.

Lim, M., Carollo, A., Bizzego, A., Chen, S. H. A., & Esposito, G. (2024). Decreased activation in left prefrontal cortex during role-play: An fNIRS study of the psychodrama sociocognitive model. *The Arts in Psychotherapy*, *87*, 102098. https://doi.org/10.1016/j.aip.2023.102098.

Lin, Y., Hsu, C.-C., Lin, C.-J. et al. (2023). Neurobiological mechanisms of dialectical behavior therapy and Morita therapy, two psychotherapies inspired by Zen. *Journal of Neural Transmission, 130*(8), 1077–1088. https://doi.org/10.1007/s00702-023-02644-3.

Llewelyn, S. P. (1988). Psychological therapy as viewed by clients and therapists. *British Journal of Clinical Psychology, 27*(3), 223–237. https://doi.org/10.1111/j.2044-8260.1988.tb00779.x.

Llewelyn, S. P., Elliott, R., Shapiro, D. A., Hardy, G., & Firth-Cozens, J. (1988). Client perceptions of significant events in prescriptive and exploratory periods of individual therapy. *British Journal of Clinical Psychology, 27*(2), 105–114. https://doi.org/10.1111/j.2044-8260.1988.tb00758.x.

Lyubomirsky, S., Sheldon, K. M., & Schkade, D. (2005). Pursuing happiness: The architecture of sustainable change. *Review of General Psychology, 9*(2), 111–131. https://doi.org/10.1037/1089-2680.9.2.111.

MacNair-Semands, R. R., Ogrodniczuk, J. S., & Joyce, A. S. (2010). Structure and Initial Validation of a Short Form of the Therapeutic Factors Inventory. *International Journal of Group Psychotherapy, 60*(2), 245–281. https://doi.org/10.1521/ijgp.2010.60.2.245.

Malhotra, B., Jones, L. C., Spooner, H. et al. (2024). A conceptual framework for a neurophysiological basis of art therapy for PTSD. *Frontiers in Human Neuroscience, 18*, 1–17. https://doi.org/10.3389/fnhum.2024.1351757.

Marci, C. D., Ham, J., Moran, E., & Orr, S. P. (2007). Physiologic correlates of perceived therapist empathy and social-emotional process during psychotherapy. *The Journal of Nervous and Mental Disease, 195*(2), 103–111. https://doi.org/10.1097/01.nmd.0000253731.71025.fc.

Marineau, R. (1989). *Jacob Levy Moreno, 1889-1974: Father of psychodrama, sociometry, and group psychotherapy.* Tavistock/Routledge.

Marra, M. M., Polejack, L., & Fleury, H. J. (2022). The use of psychodrama as a pedagogical strategy for the implementation of public policies in health and education. In H. J. Fleury, M. M. Marra, & O. H. Hadler (eds.), *Psychodrama in Brazil: Contemporary applications in mental health, education, and communities* (pp. 275–286). Springer. https://doi.org/10.1007/978-981-19-1832-2_22.

Martin, A., & Jackson, S. (2008). Brief approaches to assessing task absorption and enhanced subjective experience: Examining "short" and "core" flow in diverse performance domains. *Motivation and Emotion, 32*(3), 141–157. https://doi.org/10.1007/s11031-008-9094-0.

Martin, J., & Stelmaczonek, K. (1988). Participants' identification and recall of important events in counseling. *Journal of Counseling Psychology, 35*(4), 385–390. https://doi.org/10.1037/0022-0167.35.4.385.

McLeod, B. D., & Weisz, J. R. (2005). The Therapy Process Observational Coding System-Alliance Scale: Measure characteristics and prediction of outcome in usual clinical practice. *Journal of Consulting and Clinical Psychology, 73*(2), 323–333. https://doi.org/10.1037/0022-006X.73.2.323.

McNiff, S. (1979). From shamanism to art therapy. *Art Psychotherapy, 6*(3), 155–161. https://doi.org/10.1016/0090-9092(79)90039-5.

McVea, C. S., Gow, K., & Lowe, R. (2011). Corrective interpersonal experience in psychodrama group therapy: A comprehensive process analysis of significant therapeutic events. *Psychotherapy Research, 21*(4), 416–429. https://doi.org/10.1080/10503307.2011.577823.

Mead, G. H. (1967). *Mind, self, and society: From the standpoint of a social behaviorist*. University of Chicago Press.

Menninghaus, W., Wagner, V., Hanich, J. et al. (2017). The Distancing-Embracing model of the enjoyment of negative emotions in art reception. *Behav Brain Sci, 40*, e347. https://doi.org/10.1017/s0140525x17000309.

Milton, A. L., Das, R. K., & Merlo, E. (2023). The challenge of memory destabilisation: From prediction error to prior expectations and biomarkers. *Brain Research Bulletin, 194*, 100–104. https://doi.org/10.1016/j.brainresbull.2023.01.010.

Moreno, J. J. (1988). The music therapist: Creative arts therapist and contemporary shaman. *The Arts in Psychotherapy, 15*(4), 271–280. https://doi.org/10.1016/0197-4556(88)90029-9.

Moreno, J. L. (1934). *Who shall survive? A new approach to the problem of human interrelations*. Nervous and Mental Disease. https://doi.org/10.1037/10648-000.

Moreno, J. L. (1940). Mental catharsis and the psychodrama. *Sociometry, 3*(3), 209–244. https://doi.org/10.2307/2785151.

Moreno, J. L. (1941). The philosophy of the moment and the spontaneity theatre. *Sociometry, 4*(2), 205–226. https://doi.org/10.2307/2785526.

Moreno, J. L. (1942). Sociometry in action. *Sociometry, 5*(3), 298–315. https://doi.org/10.2307/2784969.

Moreno, J. L. (1943). The concept of sociodrama: A new approach to the problem of inter-cultural relations. *Sociometry, 6*(4), 434–449. https://doi.org/10.2307/2785223.

Moreno, J. L. (1949). Origins and foundations of interpersonal theory, sociometry and microsociology. *Sociometry, 12*(1/3), 235–254. https://doi.org/10.2307/2785390.

Moreno, J. L. (1953). *Who shall survive? Foundations of sociometry, group psychotherapy, and sociodrama*. Beacon House.

Moreno, J. L. (1955a). System of spontaneity-creativity-conserve, a reply to P. Sorokin. *Sociometry, 18*(4), 126–136. https://doi.org/10.2307/2785850.

Moreno, J. L. (1955b). Theory of spontaneity-creativity. *Sociometry, 18*(4), 105–118. www.jstor.org/stable/2785848.

Moreno, J. L. (1960). The principle of encounter. In J. L. Moreno (ed.), *The sociometry reader* (pp. 15–16). Free Press.

Moreno, J. L. (1962). Role theory and the emergence of self. *Group Psychotherapy, 15*(2), 114–117.

Moreno, J. L. (1964). The third psychiatric revolution and the scope of psychodrama. *Group Psychotherapy, 17*(2–3), 149–171.

Moreno, J. L. (1965). Therapeutic vehicles and the concept of surplus reality. *Group Psychotherapy, 18*(4), 211–216.

Moreno, J. L. (1969a). The concept of the Here and Now, Hie et Nunc: Small groups and their relation to action research. *Group Psychotherapy, 22*(3/4), 139–141.

Moreno, J. L. (1969b). The Viennese origins of the encounter movement, paving the way for existentialism, group psychotherapy and psychodrama. *Group Psychotherapy, 22*(1–2), 7–16.

Moreno, J. L. (1972). The religion of God-father. In P. E. Johnson (ed.), *Healer of the mind: A psychiatrist's search for faith* (pp. 197–215). Abington.

Moreno, J. L. (1974). The creativity theory of personality: Spontaneity, creativity and human potentialities. In I. A. Greenberg (ed.), *Psychodrama:Theory and therapy* (pp. 73–84). Souvenir Press.

Moreno, J. L. (1978). *Who shall survive? Foundations of sociometry, group psychotherapy and sociodrama* (3 ed.). Beacon House.

Moreno, J. L. (1994). *Psychodrama – first volume: Psychodrama and group psychotherapy* (4 ed.). American Society of Group Psychotherapy and Psychodrama. (Original work published in 1972).

Moreno, J. L. (2010). *The theatre of spontaneity* (3rd ed.). lulu.com. (Original work plublished in 1983).

Moreno, J. L. (2019). *Autobiography of a Genius*. Lulu. com.

Moreno, J. L., & Moreno, F. B. (1944). Spontaneity theory of child development. *Sociometry, 7*(2), 89–128. https://doi.org/10.2307/2785405.

Moreno, J. L., & Moreno, Z. T. (2012). *Psychodrama – third volume: Action therapy and principles of practice*. Lulu.com. (Original work published in 1975).

Moreno, Z. T. (1965). Psychodramatic rules, techniques and adjunctive methods. *Group psychotherapy, 18*(1–2), 73–86.

Moreno, Z. T. (1969a). Moreneans, the heretics of yesterday are the orthodoxy of today. *Group Psychotherapy, 22*(1–2), 1–6.

Moreno, Z. T. (1969b). Practical aspects of psychodrama. *Group psychotherapy, 22*(3–4), 213–219.

Moreno, Z. T. (2006). The significance of doubling and role-reversal for cosmic man. In T. Horvatin & E. Schreiber (eds.), *The quintessential Zerka: Writings by Zerka Toeman Moreno on psychodrama, sociometry and group psychotherapy* (pp. 55–59). Routledge. https://doi.org/10.4324/9780203782750.

Moreno, Z. T. (2012). *To dream again: A memoir*. Mental Health Resources.

Moreno, Z. T. (2013). Doubling should first be done with the body, not clever words .... *Zeitschrift für Psychodrama und Soziometrie*, *12*(2), 319–321. https://doi.org/10.1007/s11620-013-0206-9.

Moreno, Z. T., Blomkvist, L. D., & Rützel, T. (2000). *Psychodrama, surplus reality, and the art of healing*. Routledge.

Moreno, Z. T., Horvatin, T., & Schreiber, E. (2006). *The quintessential Zerka: Writings by Zerka Toeman Moreno on psychodrama, sociometry and group psychotherapy*. Routledge.

Morgan, D. L., & Morgan, R. K. (2008). *Single-case research methods for the behavioral and health sciences*. SAGE.

Morris, E., Fitzpatrick, M. R., & Renaud, J. (2016). A pan-theoretical conceptualization of client involvement in psychotherapy. *Psychotherapy Research*, *26*, 70–84. https://doi.org/10.1080/10503307.2014.935521.

Munder, T., & Barth, J. (2018). Cochrane's risk of bias tool in the context of psychotherapy outcome research. *Psychotherapy Research*, *28*(3), 347–355. https://doi.org/10.1080/10503307.2017.1411628.

Murphy, E. R. (2023). Hope and well-being. *Current Opinion in Psychology*, *50*, 101558. https://doi.org/10.1016/j.copsyc.2023.101558.

Neff, K. D. (2023). Self-compassion: Theory, method, research, and intervention. *Annual review of psychology*, *74*(1), 193–218. https://doi.org/10.1146/annurev-psych-032420-031047.

Neff, K. D., Tóth-Király, I., Knox, M. C., Kuchar, A., & Davidson, O. (2021). The development and validation of the State Self-Compassion Scale (long- and short form). *Mindfulness*, *12*(1), 121–140. https://doi.org/10.1007/s12671-020-01505-4.

Neumeier, L. M., Brook, L., Ditchburn, G., & Sckopke, P. (2017). Delivering your daily dose of well-being to the workplace: a randomized controlled trial of an online well-being programme for employees. *European Journal of Work and Organizational Psychology*, *26*(4), 555–573. https://doi.org/10.1080/1359432X.2017.1320281.

Nezu, A. M., & Nezu, C. M. (2007). *Evidence-based outcome research: A practical guide to conducting randomized controlled trials for psychosocial interventions*. Oxford University Press. https://doi.org/10.1093/med:psych/9780195304633.001.0001.

Nolte, J. (2020). *J. L. Moreno and the psychodramatic method: on the practice of psychodrama*. Routledge and Taylor & Francis Group.

O'Callaghan, C. (2012). Grounded theory in music therapy research. *Journal of Music Therapy, 49*(3), 236–277. https://doi.org/10.1093/jmt/49.3.236.

Oguzhanoglu, N. K., Sözeri-Varma, G., Karadag, F. et al. (2013). Prefrontal cortex neurochemical metabolite levels in major depression and the effects of treatment: An HMRS study. *Turkish Journal of Psychiatry, 25*(2), 75–83. https://pubmed.ncbi.nlm.nih.gov/24936754/.

Orkibi, H. (2009). Identifying psychodramatic elements and techniques in Goethe's "Lila". *The British Journal of Psychodrama and Sociodrama, 23* (2), 3–13.

Orkibi, H. (2014). Positive psychodrama with adolescents. In R. Berger (ed.), *Creation – the heart of therapy* (pp. 274–316). Ach books [in Hebrew].

Orkibi, H. (2018). The user-friendliness of drama: Implications for drama therapy and psychodrama admission and training. *The Arts in Psychotherapy, 59*, 101–108. https://doi.org/10.1016/j.aip.2018.04.004.

Orkibi, H. (2019). Positive psychodrama: A framework for practice and research. *The Arts in Psychotherapy, 66*, 101603. https://doi.org/10.1016/j.aip.2019.101603.

Orkibi, H. (2021). Creative adaptability: Conceptual framework, measurement, and outcomes in times of crisis. *Frontiers in Psychology, 11*(3695), 1–13. https://doi.org/10.3389/fpsyg.2020.588172.

Orkibi, H. (2023a). Creative adaptability: A measurable personal resource. *Creativity Research Journal*, 1–6. Advance online publication. https://doi.org/10.1080/10400419.2023.2223448.

Orkibi, H. (2023b). Positive psychodrama in organizations. In R. Reiter-Palmon & S. Hunter (eds.), *Handbook of organizational creativity: Individual and group level influences* (2nd ed., pp. 361–376). Elsevier Science & Technology.

Orkibi, H., Azoulay, B., Regev, D., & Snir, S. (2017). Adolescents' dramatic engagement predicts their in-session productive behaviors: A psychodrama change process study. *The Arts in Psychotherapy, 55*, 46–53. https://doi.org/10.1016/j.aip.2017.04.001.

Orkibi, H., Azoulay, B., Snir, S., & Regev, D. (2017). In-session behaviours and adolescents' self-concept and loneliness: A psychodrama process–outcome study. *Clinical Psychology and Psychotherapy, 24*, O1455–O1463. https://doi.org/10.1002/cpp.2103.

Orkibi, H., Ben-Eliyahu, A., Reiter-Palmon, R. et al. (2024). Creative adaptability and emotional well-being during the COVID-19 pandemic: An international study. *Psychology of Aesthetics, Creativity, and the Arts*, *18*(2), 245–255. https://doi.org/10.1037/aca0000445.

Orkibi, H., & Feniger-Schaal, R. (2019). Integrative systematic review of psychodrama psychotherapy research: Trends and methodological implications. *PLOS ONE*, *14*(2), e0212575. https://doi.org/10.1371/journal.pone.0212575.

Orkibi, H., & Keisari, S. (2023). Creative arts therapies: Processes and outcomes for emotional well-being. In J. C. Kaufman, J. D. Hoffmann, & Z. Ivcevic (eds.), *The Cambridge handbook of creativity and emotions* (pp. 411–433). Cambridge University Press. https://doi.org/10.1017/9781009031240.027.

Orkibi, H., Kiesari, S., Sajnani, N., & DeWitte, M. (2023). Effectiveness of drama-based therapies: A systematic review and meta-analysis of controlled studies. *Psychology of Aesthetics, Creativity and the Arts*, 1–18, Advance online publication. https://doi.org/10.1037/aca0000582.

Orkibi, H., & Ronen, T. (2015). High self-control protects the link between social support and positivity ratio for Israeli students exposed to contextual risk. *Journal of School Psychology*, *53*(4), 283–293. https://doi.org/10.1016/j.jsp.2015.06.001.

Orsmond, G. I., & Cohn, E. S. (2015). The distinctive features of a feasibility study: Objectives and guiding questions. *OTJR: Occupation, Participation and Health*, *35*(3), 169–177. https://doi.org/10.1177/1539449215578649.

Pang, D., & Ruch, W. (2019). Fusing character strengths and mindfulness interventions: Benefits for job satisfaction and performance. *Journal of Occupational Health Psychology*, *24*(1), 150–162. https://doi.org/10.1037/ocp0000144.

Paz, A., Rafaeli, E., Bar-Kalifa, E. et al. (2021). Intrapersonal and interpersonal vocal affect dynamics during psychotherapy. *Journal of Consulting and Clinical Psychology*, *89*(3), 227–239. https://doi.org/10.1037/ccp0000623.

Pellegrini, A. D., Dupuis, D., & Smith, P. K. (2007). Play in evolution and development. *Developmental Review*, *27*(2), 261–276. https://doi.org/10.1016/j.dr.2006.09.001.

Pendzik, S. (1988). Drama therapy as a form of modern shamanism. *The Journal of Transpersonal Psychology*, *20*(1), 81–92.

Pendzik, S. (2006). On dramatic reality and its therapeutic function in drama therapy. *The Arts in Psychotherapy*, *33*(4), 271–280. https://doi.org/10.1016/j.aip.2006.03.001.

Peterson, C. (1988). Explanatory style as a risk factor for illness. *Cognitive Therapy and Research*, *12*(2), 119–132. https://doi.org/10.1007/BF01204926.

Peterson, C., & Seligman, M. E. P. (2004). *Character strengths and virtues: A handbook and classification*. American Psychological Association.

Peugh, J. L. (2010). A practical guide to multilevel modeling. *Journal of School Psychology*, *48*(1), 85–112. https://doi.org/10.1016/j.jsp.2009.09.002.

Piaget, J. (1962). *Play, dreams, and imitation in childhood*. Norton.

Piaggio, G., Elbourne, D. R., Pocock, S. J. et al. (2012). Reporting of noninferiority and equivalence randomized trials: Extension of the CONSORT 2010 Statement. *JAMA*, *308*(24), 2594–2604. https://doi.org/10.1001/jama.2012.87802.

Preacher, K. J., Zyphur, M. J., & Zhang, Z. (2010). A general multilevel SEM framework for assessing multilevel mediation. *Psychological Methods*, *15*(3), 209–233. https://doi.org/10.1037/a0020141.

Prinz, J., Rafaeli, E., Reuter, J. K., Bar-Kalifa, E., & Lutz, W. (2022). Physiological activation and co-activation in an imagery-based treatment for test anxiety. *Psychotherapy Research*, *32*(2), 238–248. https://doi.org/10.1080/10503307.2021.1918353.

Pugh, M., & Salter, C. (2021). Positive psychotherapy with a pulse: Achieving depth through dialogue. *International Journal of Applied Positive Psychology*, *6*(3), 233–251. https://doi.org/10.1007/s41042-020-00046-4.

Ramseyer, F., & Tschacher, W. (2011). Nonverbal synchrony in psychotherapy: coordinated body movement reflects relationship quality and outcome. *Journal of Consulting and Clinical Psychology*, *79*(3), 284–295. https://doi.org/10.1037/a0023419.

Ramseyer, F. T. (2020). Motion energy analysis (MEA): A primer on the assessment of motion from video. *Journal of Counseling Psychology*, *67*(4), 536–549. https://doi.org/10.1037/cou0000407.

Rappaport, L. (2008). *Focusing-oriented art therapy: Accessing the body's wisdom and creative intelligence*. Jessica Kingsley.

Rasmussen, K. R., Stackhouse, M., Boon, S. D., Comstock, K., & Ross, R. (2019). Meta-analytic connections between forgiveness and health: The moderating effects of forgiveness-related distinctions. *Psychology & Health*, *34*(5), 515–534. https://doi.org/10.1080/08870446.2018.1545906.

Reich, C. M., Berman, J. S., Dale, R., & Levitt, H. M. (2014). Vocal synchrony in psychotherapy. *Journal of Social and Clinical Psychology*, *33*(5), 481–494. https://doi.org/10.1521/jscp.2014.33.5.481.

Reil, J. C. (1803). *Rhapsodieen über die Anwendung der psychischen Curmethode auf Geisteszerruettungen* Curtsche Buchhandlung.

Reivich, K., Gillham, J. E., Chaplin, T. M., & Seligman, M. E. P. (2023). From helplessness to optimism: The role of resilience in treating and preventing depression in youth. In S. Goldstein & R. B. Brooks (eds.), *Handbook of resilience in children* (pp. 161–174). Springer. https://doi.org/10.1007/978-3-031-14728-9_9.

Ronen, T. (2011). *The positive power of imagery: Harnessing client imagination in CBT and related therapies.* Wiley-Blackwell.

Rosenzweig, S. (1936). Some implicit common factors in diverse methods of psychotherapy. *American Journal of Orthopsychiatry, 6*(3), 412–415. https://doi.org/10.1111/j.1939-0025.1936.tb05248.x.

Rozik, E. (2002). *The roots of theatre: Rethinking ritual and other theories of origin.* University of Iowa Press. https://doi.org/10.2307/j.ctt20q1xvq.

Rubinstein, D., & Lahad, M. (2023). Fantastic reality: The role of imagination, playfulness, and creativity in healing trauma. *Traumatology, 29*(2), 102–111. https://doi.org/10.1037/trm0000376 M4 – Citavi.

Runco, M. A. (1996). Personal creativity: Definition and developmental issues. *New Directions for Child and Adolescent Development, 1996*(72), 3–30. https://doi.org/10.1002/cd.23219967203.

Runco, M. A. (2011). Personal creativity. In M. A. Runco & S. R. Pritzker (eds.), *Encyclopedia of creativity* (2nd ed., Vol. 2, pp. 220–223). Academic Press.

Runco, M. A., & Jaeger, G. J. (2012). The standard definition of creativity. *Creativity Research Journal, 24*(1), 92–96. https://doi.org/10.1080/10400419.2012.650092.

Ruscombe-King, G. (1998). The sharing. In M. Karp, P. Holmes, & K. B. Tauvon (eds.), *The handbook of psychodrama* (pp. 177–196). Routledge.

Russ, S. W. (2014). *Pretend play in childhood: Foundation of adult creativity.* American Psychological Association.

Rye, M. S., Loiacono, D. M., Folck, C. D. et al. (2001). Evaluation of the psychometric properties of two forgiveness scales. *Current Psychology: A Journal for Diverse Perspectives on Diverse Psychological Issues, 20*(3), 260–277. https://doi.org/10.1007/s12144-001-1011-6.

Sarbin, T., & Allen, V. (1968). Role theory. In L. Gardner & A. Elliot (eds.), *The handbook of social psychology* (2 ed., Vol. 1, pp. 488–567). Addison-Wesley.

Scarinzi, A. (2015). *Aesthetics and the embodied mind: Beyond art theory and the cartesian mind-body dichotomy.* Springer.

Schechner, R., & Brady, S. (2013). *Performance studies: An introduction* (3rd ed.). Routledge.

Scheier, M. F., Carver, C. S., & Bridges, M. W. (1994). Distinguishing optimism from neuroticism (and trait anxiety, self-mastery, and self-esteem): A reevaluation of the life orientation test. *Journal of Personality and Social*

Psychology, *67*(6), 1063–1078. https://doi.org/10.1037/0022-3514.67.6.1063.

Schmais, C. (1988). Creative arts therapies and shamanism: A comparison. *The Arts in Psychotherapy*, *15*(4), 281–284. https://doi.org/10.1016/0197-4556(88)90030-5.

Schulz, K. F., Altman, D. G., & Moher, D. (2010). CONSORT 2010 statement: Updated guidelines for reporting parallel group randomised trials. *Journal of Pharmacology and Pharmacotherapeutics*, *1*(2), 100–107. https://doi.org/10.4103/0976-500X.72352.

Scorolli, C. (2019). Re-enacting the bodily self on stage: Embodied cognition meets psychoanalysis. *Frontiers in Psychology*, *10*, 1–18. https://doi.org/10.3389/fpsyg.2019.00492.

Shechtman, Z., & Leichtentritt, J. (2010). The association of process with outcomes in child group therapy. *Psychotherapy Research*, *20*, 8–21. https://doi.org/10.1080/10503300902926562.

Sheldon, K. M., & Lyubomirsky, S. (2021). Revisiting the sustainable happiness model and pie chart: can happiness be successfully pursued? *The Journal of Positive Psychology*, *16*(2), 145–154. https://doi.org/10.1080/17439760.2019.1689421.

Shen, X., & Masek, L. (2024). The playful mediator, moderator, or outcome? An integrative review of the roles of play and playfulness in adult-centered psychological interventions for mental health. *The Journal of Positive Psychology*, *19*(6), 1037–1050. https://doi.org/10.1080/17439760.2023.2288955.

Siegel, D. J. (1999). *The developing mind: Toward a neurobiology of interpersonal experience*. Guilford Press.

Sin, N., & Lyubomirsky, S. (2009). Enhancing well-being and reducing depressive symptoms with positive psychology interventions: A practice-friendly meta-analysis. *Journal of Clinical Psychology: In Session*, *65*, 467–487.

Skivington, K., Matthews, L., Simpson, S. A. et al. (2021). A new framework for developing and evaluating complex interventions: update of Medical Research Council guidance. *BMJ*, *374*, n2061. https://doi.org/10.1136/bmj.n2061.

Skottnik, L., & Linden, D. E. J. (2019). Mental imagery and brain regulation—new links between psychotherapy and neuroscience. *Frontiers in Psychiatry*, *10*, 1–14. https://doi.org/10.3389/fpsyt.2019.00779.

Skov, M., & Nadal, M. (2022). *The Routledge international handbook of neuroaesthetics*. Taylor & Francis Group.

Slivjak, E. T., Kirk, A., & Arch, J. J. (2023). The psychophysiology of self-compassion. In A. Finlay-Jones, K. Bluth, & K. Neff (eds.), *Handbook of self-compassion* (pp. 291–307). Springer International Publishing. https://doi.org/10.1007/978-3-031-22348-8_17.

Smith, J. K., & Smith, L. F. (2017). The nature of creativity: Mayflies, octopi, and the best bad idea we have. In R. A. Beghetto & B. Sriraman (eds.), *Creative contradictions in education* (pp. 21–35). Springer.

Smith, P., Caputi, P., & Crittenden, N. (2013). Measuring optimism in organizations: Development of a workplace explanatory style questionnaire. *Journal of Happiness Studies*, *4*(2), 415–432. https://doi.org/10.1007/s10902-012-9336-4.

Snow, S. (2009). Ritual/theatre/therapy. In D. R. Johnson & R. Emunah (eds.), *Current approaches in drama therapy* (2nd ed., pp. 117–144). C. C. Thomas.

Snyder, C. R. (2000). *Handbook of hope: Theory, measures & applications*. Academic Press.

Snyder, C. R. (2002). TARGET ARTICLE: Hope theory: Rainbows in the mind. *Psychological Inquiry*, *13*(4), 249–275. https://doi.org/10.1207/s15327965pli1304_01.

Soysal, F. S. Ö. (2023). The effects of psychodrama on emotion regulation skills in emerging adults. *Current Psychology*, *42*(6), 4469–4482. https://doi.org/10.1007/s12144-021-01800-w.

Spence, J. R., Brown, D. J., Keeping, L. M., & Lian, H. (2014). Helpful today, but not tomorrow? Feeling grateful as a predictor of daily organizational citizenship behaviors. *Personnel Psychology*, *67*(3), 705–738. https://doi.org/10.1111/peps.12051.

Steffen, P. R., Bartlett, D., Channell, R. M. et al. (2021). Integrating breathing techniques into psychotherapy to improve HRV: Which approach is best? *Frontiers in Psychology*, *12*, 1–11. https://doi.org/10.3389/fpsyg.2021.624254.

Tarashoeva, G., Marinova-Djambazova, P., & Ilieva, K. (2022). Therapeutic factors and therapeutic techniques in psychodrama. *Academic Journal of Creative Arts Therapies*, *22*(1), 477–488. https://ajcat.haifa.ac.il/index.php/en/2011-02-01-08-53-39/volume-12-issue-1-june-2022.

Tarashoeva, G., Marinova-Djambazova, P., & Kojuharov, H. (2017). Effectiveness of psychodrama therapy in patients with panic disorders: Final results. *International Journal of Psychotherapy*, *21*(2), 55–66.

Tassinary, L. G., Hess, U., & Carcoba, L. M. (2012). Peripheral physiological measures of psychological constructs. In *APA handbook of research methods in psychology, Vol 1: Foundations, planning, measures, and psychometrics* (pp. 461–488). American Psychological Association. https://doi.org/10.1037/13619-025.

Tate, R. L., Perdices, M., Rosenkoetter, U. et al. (2016). The single-case reporting guideline In behavioural interventions (SCRIBE) 2016: Explanation and elaboration. *Archives of Scientific Psychology*, *4*(1), 10–31. https://doi.org/10.1037/arc0000027.

Tauvon, K. B. (1998). Principles of psychodrama. In M. Karp, P. Holmes, & K. B. Tauvon (eds.), *The handbook of psychodrama* (pp. 31–49). Routledge.

Taylor, M. (ed.). (2013). *The oxford handbook of the development of imagination*. Oxford University Press. https://doi.org/10.1093/oxfordhb/9780195395761.001.0001.

Thoits, P. A. (2011). Mechanisms linking social ties and support to physical and mental health. *Journal of Health and Social Behavior*, *52*(2), 145–161. https://doi.org/10.1177/0022146510395592.

Timulak, L. (2008). *Research in psychotherapy and counselling*. SAGE.

Timulak, L. (2010). Significant events in psychotherapy: An update of research findings. *Psychology and Psychotherapy: Theory, Research and Practice*, *83*(4), 421–447. https://doi.org/10.1348/147608310X499404.

Tomashin, A., Gordon, I., & Wallot, S. (2022). Interpersonal physiological synchrony predicts group cohesion. *Frontiers in Human Neuroscience*, *16*, 1–12. https://doi.org/10.3389/fnhum.2022.903407.

Tomasulo, D. J. (2019). The virtual gratitude visit (VGV): Using psychodrama and role-playing as a positive intervention. In L. E. Van Zyl & S. Rothmann Sr (eds.), *Positive Psychological Intervention Design and Protocols for Multi-Cultural Contexts* (pp. 405–413). Springer. https://doi.org/10.1007/978-3-030-20020-6_18.

Uchino, B. N., Bowen, K., Carlisle, M., & Birmingham, W. (2012). Psychological pathways linking social support to health outcomes: A visit with the "ghosts" of research past, present, and future. *Social Science & Medicine*, *74*(7), 949–957. https://doi.org/10.1016/j.socscimed.2011.11.023.

Vaisvaser, S. (2021). The embodied-enactive-interactive brain: Bridging neuroscience and creative arts therapies. *Frontiers in Psychology*, *12*, 1–13. https://doi.org/10.3389/fpsyg.2021.634079.

Vaisvaser, S., King, J. L., Orkibi, H., & Aleem, H. (2024). Neurodynamics of relational aesthetic engagement in creative arts therapies. *Review of General Psychology*, *28*(3), 203–218. https://doi.org/10.1177/10892680241260840.

van der Kolk, B. A. (2014). *The body keeps the score: Brain, mind, and body in the healing of trauma*. Viking.

Vygotsky, L. (1966). Play and its role in the mental development of the child. *Soviet psychology*, *5*(3), 6–18. www.marxists.org/archive/vygotsky/works/1933/play.htm.

Wampold, B. E. (2015). How important are the common factors in psychotherapy? An update. *World Psychiatry*, *14*(3), 270–277. https://doi.org/10.1002/wps.20238.

Wessler, J., Gebhard, P., & Zilcha-Mano, S. (2024). Investigating movement synchrony in therapeutic settings using socially interactive agents: An experimental toolkit. *Frontiers in Psychiatry*, *15*, 1–5. https://doi.org/10.3389/fpsyt.2024.1330158.

Wilkins, P. (1999). *Psychodrama*. SAGE.

Winnicott, D. W. (1980). *Playing and reality*. Tavistock.

World Health Organization. (1948). WHO Constitution. www.who.int/about/governance/constitution.

Worthington, E. L., Witvliet, C. V. O., Pietrini, P., & Miller, A. J. (2007). Forgiveness, health, and well-being: A review of evidence for emotional versus decisional forgiveness, dispositional forgivingness, and reduced unforgiveness. *Journal of Behavioral Medicine*, *30*(4), 291–302. https://doi.org/10.1007/s10865-007-9105-8.

Yablonsky, L. (1954). The future-projection technique. *Group Psychotherapy*, *7*(3–4), 303–305.

Yalom, I. D., & Leszcz, M. (2005). *The theory and practice of group psychotherapy* (5th ed.). Basic Books.

Yaniv, D. (2011). Revisiting Morenian psychodramatic encounter in light of contemporary neuroscience: Relationship between empathy and creativity. *The Arts in Psychotherapy*, *38*(1), 52–58. https://doi.org/10.1016/j.aip.2010.12.001.

Zaccaro, A., Piarulli, A., Laurino, M. et al. (2018). How breath-control can change your life: A systematic review on psycho-physiological correlates of slow breathing. *Frontiers in Human Neuroscience*, *12*, 1–16. https://doi.org/10.3389/fnhum.2018.00353.

Zhang, Y., Meng, T., Hou, Y., Pan, Y., & Hu, Y. (2018). Interpersonal brain synchronization associated with working alliance during psychological counseling. *Psychiatry Research: Neuroimaging*, *282*, 103–109. https://doi.org/10.1016/j.pscychresns.2018.09.007.

Zilcha-Mano, S. (2024). How getting in sync is curative: Insights gained from research in psychotherapy. *Psychological Review*, 1–18. Advance online publication. https://doi.org/10.1037/rev0000471.

Zilcha-Mano, S., Shamay-Tsoory, S., Dolev-Amit, T., Zagoory-Sharon, O., & Feldman, R. (2020). Oxytocin as a biomarker of the formation of therapeutic alliance in psychotherapy and counseling psychology. *Journal of Counseling Psychology*, *67*(4), 523–535. https://doi.org/10.1037/cou0000386.

Cambridge Elements

Creativity and Imagination

Anna Abraham
University of Georgia, USA

Anna Abraham, Ph.D. is the E. Paul Torrance Professor at the University of Georgia, USA. Her educational and professional training has been within the disciplines of psychology and neuroscience, and she has worked across a diverse range of academic departments and institutions the world over, all of which have informed her cross-cultural and multidisciplinary focus. She has penned numerous publications including the 2018 book, *The Neuroscience of Creativity* (Cambridge University Press), and 2020 edited volume, *The Cambridge Handbook of the Imagination*. Her latest book is *The Creative Brain: Myths and Truths* (2024, MIT Press).

About the Series

Cambridge Elements in Creativity and Imagination publishes original perspectives and insightful reviews of empirical research, methods, theories, or applications in the vast fields of creativity and the imagination. The series is particularly focused on showcasing novel, necessary and neglected perspectives.

Cambridge Elements

Creativity and Imagination

Elements in the Series

There's No Such Thing as Creativity: How Plato and 20th Century Psychology Have Misled Us
John Baer

Slow Wonder: Letters on Imagination and Education
Peter O'Connor and Claudia Rozas Gómez

Prophets at a Tangent: How Art Shapes Social Imagination
Geoff Mulgan

Visions and Decisions: Imagination and Technique in Music Composition
Bruce Adolphe

Item-Response Theory for Creativity Measurement
Nils Myszkowski

Design Thinking and Other Approaches: How Different Disciplines See, Think and Act
Nathan Crilly

Connective Creativity: What Art Can Teach Us About Collaboration
Austin Choi-Fitzpatrick and Gordon Hoople

Landscapes of the Imagination
Gerald C. Cupchik

Outsight: Restoring the Role of Objects in Creative Problem Solving
Frédéric Vallée-Tourangeau

Narrative Creativity: An Introduction to How and Why
Angus Fletcher and Mike Benveniste

Mechanisms of Change and Creativity in Nature and Culture
Arne Dietrich

Psychodrama: A Creative Method to Survive and Thrive
Hod Orkibi

A full series listing is available at: www.cambridge.org/ECAI

For EU product safety concerns, contact us at Calle de José Abascal, 56–1°, 28003 Madrid, Spain or eugpsr@cambridge.org.

www.ingramcontent.com/pod-product-compliance
Ingram Content Group UK Ltd.
Pitfield, Milton Keynes, MK11 3LW, UK
UKHW020252130925
462879UK00021B/644